## DATE DUE

| | |
|---|---|
| | |
| | |
| | |
| | |
| | |
| | |
| | |
| | |
| | |
| | |
| | |
| | |
| | |
| | |
| | |
| | |

COMPREHENSIVE RESEARCH
AND STUDY GUIDE

# BLOOM'S
## MAJOR
## DRAMATISTS

*Neil*
*Simon*

EDITED AND WITH AN
INTRODUCTION BY HAROLD BLOOM

## BLOOM'S MAJOR DRAMATISTS

Aeschylus

Anton Chekhov

Aristophanes

Berthold Brecht

Euripides

Henrik Ibsen

Ben Johnson

Christopher Marlowe

Arthur Miller

Eugene O'Neill

Shakespeare's Comedies

Shakespeare's Histories

Shakespeare's Romances

Shakespeare's Tragedies

George Bernard Shaw

Neil Simon

Sophocles

Tennessee Williams

August Wilson

## BLOOM'S MAJOR NOVELISTS

Jane Austen

The Brontës

Willa Cather

Stephen Crane

Charles Dickens

Fyodor Dostoevsky

William Faulkner

F. Scott Fitzgerald

Thomas Hardy

Nathaniel Hawthorne

Ernest Hemingway

Henry James

James Joyce

D. H. Lawrence

Toni Morrison

John Steinbeck

Stendhal

Leo Tolstoy

Mark Twain

Alice Walker

Edith Wharton

Virginia Woolf

## BLOOM'S MAJOR WORLD POETS

Geoffrey Chaucer

Emily Dickinson

John Donne

T. S. Eliot

Robert Frost

Langston Hughes

John Milton

Edgar Allan Poe

Shakespeare's Poems & Sonnets

Alfred, Lord Tennyson

Walt Whitman

William Wordsworth

## BLOOM'S MAJOR SHORT STOR WRITERS

William Faulkner

F. Scott Fitzgerald

Ernest Hemingway

O. Henry

James Joyce

Herman Melville

Flannery O'Connor

Edgar Allan Poe

J. D. Salinger

John Steinbeck

Mark Twain

Eudora Welty

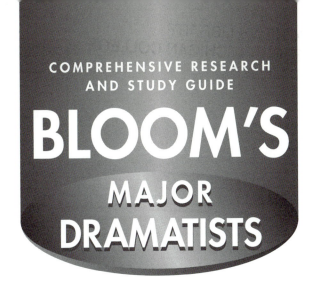

COMPREHENSIVE RESEARCH
AND STUDY GUIDE

# BLOOM'S
## MAJOR
## DRAMATISTS

# *Neil*
# *Simon*

EDITED AND WITH AN INTRODUCTION
BY HAROLD BLOOM

© 2002 by Chelsea House Publishers, a subsidiary of
Haights Cross Communications.

Introduction © 2002 by Harold Bloom.

Printed and bound in the United States of America.

First Printing
1 3 5 7 9 8 6 4 2

Library of Congress Cataloging-in-Publication Data
Neil Simon / edited and with an introduction by Harold Bloom.
        p. cm. — (Bloom's major dramatists)
    Includes bibliographical references and index.
    ISBN 0-7910-6360-7 (alk. paper)
        1. Simon, Neil. Criticism and interpretation. I. Bloom, Harold.
    II. Series.
    PS3537.I663 Z789    2001
    812'.54—dc21                                2001042335

Chelsea House Publishers
1974 Sproul Road, Suite 400
Broomall, PA 19008-0914

The Chelsea House World Wide Web address is
http://www.chelseahouse.com

Series Editor: Matt Uhler
Contributing Editor: Anne Marie Albertazzi

Produced for Chelsea House Publishers by:
Robert Gerson Publisher's Services, Santa Barbara, CA

# Contents

# User's Guide

This volume is designed to present biographical, critical, and bibliographical information on the author's best-known or most important works. Following Harold Bloom's editor's note and introduction is a detailed biography of the author, discussing major life events and important literary accomplishments. A plot summary of each play follows, tracing significant themes, patterns, and motifs in the work.

A selection of critical extracts, derived from previously published material from leading critics, analyzes aspects of each play. The extracts consist of statements from the author, if available, early reviews of the work, and later evaluations up to the present. A bibliography of the author's writings (including a complete list of all works written, cowritten, edited, and translated), a list of additional books and articles on the author and his or her work, and an index of themes and ideas in the author's writings conclude the volume.

~

**Harold Bloom** is Sterling Professor of the Humanities at Yale University and Henry W. and Albert A. Berg Professor of English at the New York University Graduate School. He is the author of over 20 books, including *Shelley's Mythmaking* (1959), *The Visionary Company* (1961), *Blake's Apocalypse* (1963), *Yeats* (1970), *A Map of Misreading* (1975), *Kabbalah and Criticism* (1975), *Agon: Toward a Theory of Revisionism* (1982), *The American Religion* (1992), *The Western Canon* (1994), and *Omens of Millennium: The Gnosis of Angels, Dreams, and Resurrection* (1996). *The Anxiety of Influence* (1973) sets forth Professor Bloom's provocative theory of the literary relationships between the great writers and their predecessors. His most recent books include *Shakespeare: The Invention of the Human*, a 1998 National Book Award finalist, and *How to Read and Why*, which was published in 2000.

Professor Bloom earned his Ph.D. from Yale University in 1955 and has served on the Yale faculty since then. He is a 1985 MacArthur Foundation Award recipient, served as the Charles Eliot Norton Professor of Poetry at Harvard University in 1987–88, and has received honorary degrees from the universities of Rome and Bologna. In 1999, Professor Bloom received the prestigious American Academy of Arts and Letters Gold Medal for Criticism.

Currently, Harold Bloom is the editor of numerous Chelsea House volumes of literary criticism, including the series BLOOM'S NOTES, BLOOM'S MAJOR DRAMATISTS, BLOOM'S MAJOR NOVELISTS, MAJOR LITERARY CHARACTERS, MODERN CRITICAL VIEWS, MODERN CRITICAL INTERPRETATIONS, and WOMEN WRITERS OF ENGLISH AND THEIR WORKS.

# Editor's Note

My Introduction centers upon the aesthetic status of Neil Simon's plays as skilled "period pieces."

Norman Nadel comments on the vivacity of *The Odd Couple*, while John McClain shrewdly observes the displacement of marital roles in Simon's play. The question of Simon's enormous appeal is considered by Howard Taubman, whose observations are reinforced by Edythe M. McGovern on the quest for concord. Richard Grayson accurately indicates the absence of any homoerotic undersong in the play.

*Plaza Suite* is considered mostly as theater by Clive Barnes, Walter Kerr, Martin Gottfried and Richard P. Cooke. William Goldman deprecates Simon's overt and deliberate cheerfulness, while Edythe M. McGovern finds more verisimilitude in the farce's characters than I am able to perceive.

*The Sunshine Boys* properly provokes more serious reflections, as in Martin Gottfried's wistfulness at Simon's lost potential, and the observations by Edwin Wilson and Sheila Ennis Geitner on the play's underlying pathos. The legacy of Yiddish theater is explored directly by Daniel Walden and Ellen Schiff, while C. W. E. Bigsby illuminates the issue of ambivalence.

*Lost in Yonkers*, a drama that is itself a missed opportunity, is chided gently by Frank Rich for its sliding over familial cruelty, while Clive Barnes rightly questions the play's happy ending, and Howard Kissel meditates upon Jewish themes of survival through self-sacrifice. Jack Kroll investigates the autobiographical aspects of the play. Ellen Schiff, compassionately considering the dreadful grandmother's past, and Bette Mandl more generally, invoke the Holocaust as the play's dwarfing context.

# Introduction

## HAROLD BLOOM

At his best, Neil Simon moves towards a Chekhovian controlled pathos, but only rarely does he approach close to it. His comedy essentially is situational, though the overtones of Jewish traditional folk humor sometimes allow him to suggest a darker strain. He is a popular playmaker of enormous skill, and certainly persuades more easily on the stage and the screen than he does in print. If all aesthetic criteria were indeed societal, as our debased academies now tell us, then Simon would be more than an eminent hand. His plays are honorable period pieces, and will have the fate of Pinero and Odets, dramatists of their moment. And yet, there is a normative quality in his work that is heartening, and that always promises a touch more than he needs to give.

Writing what is essentially Jewish comedy after the Holocaust is not exactly an unmixed enterprise, and there is a deft quickness in Simon's rhetoric that is admirably sustained, doubtless reflecting his training as a television gag-writer. Though *Lost in Yonkers* is his sharpest and most mature play, it is marred by a forced, relatively happy ending, which has the effect of rendering the entire drama rather questionable.

*The Odd Couple* has entered popular consciousness, but is perhaps too overtly psychological to endure beyond our era. *Plaza Suite* can cause one to wince, in tribute to its truth-telling, but its fundamental slightness is too apparent. It is *The Sunshine Boys,* for all its sentimentality, that may last longest. Willie Clark and Al Lewis are nowhere as funny as Joe Smith and Charlie Dale, probably the greatest Jewish vaudevillians, but their ambivalent relationship is rendered as precisely representative of the complex feelings evoked by Yiddish popular culture as it transformed into the entertainment industry of American Jewry.

Neil Simon is the most popular contemporary American playwright, with a larger audience than Arthur Miller, Edward Albee, August Wilson, Tony Kushner and other real talents. It would be difficult to compare him favorably to any of them, because his range is narrow, and his mode is so deliberately restrictive. He fades away absolutely if we invoke *Death of a Salesman, The Zoo Story, Joe Turner's Come and Gone,* or *Angels in America.* And yet he is a grand entertainer, and at least in *The Sunshine Boys,* something more than that. Yiddish theater, on which I was raised, goes on more absolutely in Kushner and in David Mamet, but it finds a nostalgic echo, ebbing but sometimes poignant, in Neil Simon's comedies. ❀

# Biography of Neil Simon

Marvin Neil Simon was born on July 4, 1927 in the Bronx, New York. He grew up in Washington Heights, at the northern tip of Manhattan with his father Irving Simon, a garment salesman, his mother Mamie Simon, and his older brother Danny. Simon's comic awareness developed from a very young age; his family nicknamed him "Doc" because he loved to brandish his toy stethoscope, and he was thrown out of movie theaters for laughing too loud. At sixteen, Simon graduated from DeWitt Clinton High School and went on to study engineering at New York University in the United States Army Air Force Reserve program. He completed his basic training in Biloxi, Mississippi and was stationed at Lowry Field, Colorado where he worked as sports editor for the Army newspaper *Rev-Meter*. Simon was discharged as a corporal in 1946.

Back in New York, Simon worked in the mailroom of Warner Brothers' East Coast office, while his brother Danny Simon worked in the publicity department. The two brothers joined their talents for fifteen years to write comedy scripts for radio and television. They created scripts for the radio personality Goodman Ace and worked alongside Woody Allen, Mel Brooks and Larry Gelbart on *The Phil Silvers Show* and Sid Caesar's *Your Show of Shows*. In addition, they wrote for Jackie Gleason and the "Red Buttons Show," among others. In 1952 and 1953, Neil and Danny wrote sketches for amateur theater in Pennsylvania which later became *Catch a Star!* on the professional stage in 1955. In the late 1950s, Danny Simon began a new career as a television director, while "Doc" struck out on his own as a writer, receiving several Emmy nominations for his work on the "Sid Caesar Show" (1957) and the "Garry Moore Show" (1959).

Simon left television and began writing for the theater, which afforded him a larger range of artistic freedom. His first play, *Come Blow Your Horn* (1960) ran for two years on Broadway. From then on his work for the stage enjoyed unprecedented commercial success. *Barefoot in the Park* (1963), his most popular play, ran for over 1,500 performances on Broadway. Simon virtually dominated Broadway: *Barefoot in the Park, The Odd Couple, Sweet Charity,* and

*The Star-Spangled Girl* all ran simultaneously during the 1966–67 season, while *Plaza Suite, Last of the Red Hot Lovers,* and *Promises, Promises* were all on stage during the 1970–71 season.

As Julius Novic wrote in *The Humanist* in 1976, "The problem with Simon for serious critics is that he is good enough to make them angry that he isn't better." Despite his enormous popular success, many critics were dismissing Simon as a mere writer of jokes, accusing him of hindering dramatic character development with incessant one-liners. Yet, his autobiographical trilogy *Brighton Beach Memoirs* (1982), *Biloxi Blues* (1984), *and Broadway Bound* (1986) changed the tide of opinion among critics. These plays received accolades for their warmth, wisdom, realism, and depth. Loosely based on Simon's own childhood, Army service, and early television career, these plays impressed critics as more organically structured than his early plays. He was praised for outgrowing one-liners to portray moments of suffering characterized by a new brand of melancholy wit.

On June 29, 1983, Neil Simon became the first living playwright to have a theatre named after him; and in the years following he received even higher honors. *Lost in Yonkers* won a Pulitzer Prize for Drama and a Tony Award for best drama in 1991. In addition, *The Odd Couple* and *Biloxi Blues* have received Tony Awards for best play. Simon has had more plays adapted to film than any other American playwright, and his screenplays *The Odd Couple* (1968), *The Sunshine Boys* (1975) and *California Suite* (1978) have all received Academy Award Nominations. He has also written many original screenplays; of these, *The Goodbye Girl* won a 1978 Golden Globe Award. Simon has also won the special Tony Award for overall contributions to the theater, the Writers Guild Award, the Evening Standard Award, the New York Drama Critics Circle Award, the Sam S. Shubert Foundation Award, the Outer Circle Award, and others.

Though reviews of his plays have always been mixed, he has been noted for his ability to see humor in the tiresome and often tragic neuroses of human relationships. As in plays like *Barefoot in the Park* and *The Odd Couple*, which each feature an impulsive hedonist and a rigid conformer, he often pits opposing character types against each other in order to laugh at what happens when they share a small space. Simon's humorous take on human suffering has been seen as both compassionate and superficial, both timeless and bourgeois. As

Edwin Wilson of the *Wall Street Journal* wrote in 1976, "In showing us the pain of his characters Mr. Simon demonstrates once again how well he understands one of the secrets of comedy: that for human beings the funny bone is often found near a raw nerve, and that when we look through a comic prism we are likely to laugh the hardest when others suffer the most."

In a 1997 interview with *Stage & Screen,* Simon gave his impression of the ways in which Broadway has changed since his heyday: "Broadway has turned into Hollywood in a way. . . . People coming from out of town want to see a spectacle, something like *Titanic.* . . . It's only once in a while that a really good play comes to New York. . . . In that respect, I'm glad I was born when I was born." *The Dinner Party,* Simon's current play on Broadway, is an experimental mixture of farce and serious drama set in Paris. ❀

# Plot Summary of
## *The Odd Couple*

Neil Simon got the story for *The Odd Couple* from his brother Danny Simon, whose experience of divorce prompted him to ask the question "What's funny about divorce?" Neil Simon's play is certainly one answer to that question: it brings together in close quarters two lonely men who have been left by their wives, and in doing so, it dramatizes how they inflict on each other the same character flaws that drove their wives away in the first place. Clearly, neither Felix nor Oscar has learned from his mistakes, and to emphasize this, Simon throws their foibles into high relief. As the critic Sheila Ennis Geitner explains, "Much of the humor in *The Odd Couple* is achieved through exaggeration: Felix and Oscar are stylized characters; Felix's grief is overblown; the poker players are caricatures . . . Simon makes the absurd believable, and the audience can see parts of themselves in Felix and Oscar" (*Dictionary of Literary Biography* 7, p. 255). Because Felix and Oscar are each other's opposites, they become each other's worst nightmares; and as in a bad marriage, they must separate when no compromise is reached. In the meantime, the slovenly, jaded Oscar and the punctilious, hypersensitive Felix bicker over stray crumbs and a tardy arrival to dinner just as any married couple would. Neil Simon originally envisioned this play as a dark comedy, and while his talent lies in making light of stark realities like mid-life loneliness, he is equally adept at darkening a funny moment like Felix's spoon-waving with the bleak suggestion of inescapability and infinite repetition.

**Act One** begins with a poker game between Murray, Roy, Speed, Vinnie and Oscar on a Friday night. Oscar's apartment, described as not having benefited from a woman's touch in three months, has become a men-only haven where anything goes. Free from the responsibility that goes with marriage, the poker players can be as messy and crude as they like. Oscar leaves a trail of cigar ashes, chips, spilled beer and dirty dishes behind him without so much as a look back, and his married friends seem comforted by this. During the poker game, the men's banter serves to introduce us to their characters and main preoccupations. Roy, Oscar's accountant, reminds him that despite being one of the highest paid sports writers in New York, Oscar still manages to be in debt to the government, his wife, and his friends. Murray, a cop, has a fixation on the time which reflects how much his wife nags him about staying out too late. Speed is a consummate complainer, and Vinnie is so cheap that he takes his family to Florida in July, when no one is there, to get a discount on the hotel room. During the poker game, the men poke fun at each other's flaws both bitterly and affectionately. Oscar's son calls to ask after the goldfish he has left in the apartment, but Oscar does not have the heart to tell him that it has died of neglect. Oscar's ex-wife Blanche gets on the phone to ask after her alimony. Again, Oscar has not been able to deliver; he seems only to be able to live in the moment.

Meanwhile, the men are worried about Felix, who has never once been late to a poker game. Felix, a fastidious creature of habit, is the sort of man who wears a vest and galoshes, wears a seat belt during a drive-in movie, and cleans out ashtrays; no one can believe he would stand them up. Murray's wife calls to reveal that Felix and his wife Frances have split up after 12 years, and now Felix, who has threatened to commit suicide, is missing. Felix shows up at the door, and though the others pretend they do not know what has happened, they are anxious about preventing any suicidal behavior. He goes into the bathroom to cry, then complains that his stomach bothers him, due to his swallowing a whole bottle of his wife's green pills. Melodramatic and self-martyring by nature, Felix gets the attention he desires.

After the others leave, Felix has a neck spasm and Oscar tries to alleviate it by rubbing it. Oscar finds Felix "panicky" with a "low threshold for composure", noting that he is the only man he knows with "clenched hair." Nevertheless, he proposes that Felix move in with him as a way of getting over his wife. Using his own experience of being left by his wife, Oscar tells him that even though the fact of being alone "hits you in the face like a wet glove every night," Felix ought to face facts, stop crying, and have a drink. Felix admits to being a poor living partner: he has terrible allergies to his wife's perfume, obsessively records expenses, cleans up after her and the maid, and re-seasons her food after she cooks. A master at self-pity, he hates himself for all his faults but cannot fathom living without his wife and kids. When Frances calls to ask Oscar when Felix will move his clothes so she can repaint the room, Felix realizes that the marriage is indeed over.

At another poker game two weeks later (**Act Two, Scene One**) we see that Felix's immaculate standards have invaded the apartment and utterly transformed it. Felix's infuriatingly fastidious behavior, despite its dire marital consequences, has not changed at all. Poker nights are not the same anymore since this domestic lunatic has been hovering over them and cleaning up after their every crumb. Speed, the most disgruntled of them all, says he refuses to give up his Friday nights to watch cooking and housekeeping. The game ends early. When the guests have left, Oscar confronts Felix about his excessive cleaning and tells him to "let loose," stop trying to control everything, and express his anger. Felix throws a cup across the room, only to complain that it hurt his arm. Oscar's solution to the rising tension is to find dates for the two of them. He convinces Felix to agree to a double date with two sisters who live in the building, and he makes Felix promise to have a good time. Ironically, Oscar is convinced that if anything can break Felix out of his prudish and meticulous mindset, it is a woman.

A few days later (**Scene Two**), it is the night of the big date. Felix chastises Oscar for arriving home late and complains frantically that his dinner will be ruined because the guests will arrive later than the London Broil will finish cooking. The squabble that results is a showpiece of Simon's extraordinary ability to capture those classic moments of ordinary experience. Simon has been called a writer for the middle class, and this scene is funny precisely because it allows the audience, no matter what their marital status, to see themselves in Felix and Oscar. Felix does not adhere to strict gender stereotypes, so this scene translates to any situation in which two supposedly compatible people end up under one roof. As the critic Edythe M. McGovern argues, "the playwright has significantly altered his previously held position regarding innate sexual differences, a position which he was probably quite unaware of having before creating *The Odd Couple*."

When Cecily and Gwendolyn Pigeon arrive, Felix is extremely awkward and can only think of the London Broil. As Oscar is in the kitchen happily making drinks, Felix manages to make the two sisters cry right along with him as he laments the loss of his wife and children. Oscar is shocked to see the change in mood when he returns with the drinks. Felix has forgotten about the London Broil and it is burned to a crisp. The sisters, whose hearts have been touched by Felix, suggest going to their apartment, which Oscar considers a coup. He is willing to accept any invitation, even if a grown man's tears are necessary to accomplish it. Felix, however, will not go because all this sorrow has shown him how emotionally tied he is to his wife and children. Oscar is horrified: Felix is the lynchpin to this potentially successful date. When a disgusted Oscar leaves to meet the sisters on his own, he asks Felix if this is the way he intends to live the rest of his life, to which Felix responds "we are what we are."

The next evening (**Act Three**), Oscar is not speaking to Felix. He has spent the previous evening drinking tea with the Pigeon sisters and telling Felix's life story. Oscar deliberately messes up the apartment, then throws Felix's dish of home-cooked spaghetti across the room. Felix's irritating behavior has brought Oscar to the breaking point; crazed, he demands that Felix move out and give him his freedom. Felix agrees to leave, but tells Oscar that "it will be on your head." This is truly the curse of the martyr, and it troubles Oscar so much that he is willing to work things out with Felix. However, Felix has already made up his mind to leave.

Oscar's poker friends arrive, and when they hear what has happened, they are not surprised. Murray claims Felix causes his own grief by irritating people that he lives with; it is a repetitive pattern that will always get him kicked out. Then the Pigeon sisters arrive with Felix in tow. They are his new champions; they want him to get his clothes so he can move in with them until he finds a place. He agrees, and in his martyr's way, tells the boys they can leave all the crumbs they want from now on.

At the end of the play, it is clear that each man has benefited from the other's personality; yet only after they "break up" can this benefit be seen. For Felix, this change is borne out when the phone rings. Believing his wife is on the phone for him, Felix refuses to talk to her until he can approach her with some dignity. The same man who pined inconsolably over the loss of his wife seems ready to face her more calmly. However, it turns out not to be Felix's wife but Oscar's wife on the phone. Oscar's conversation with her reveals how living with Felix has forced him to organize his expenses and become more responsible. He has caught up on his alimony payments and sent a new goldfish to his son to replace the one his poor housekeeping habits killed. As Felix leaves, Oscar is warning his poker buddies not to get ashes on the carpet.

Though these two men will most likely never be able to live together again and will probably never change their essential characters, their opposing personalities seem to have found a middle ground, if perhaps only for a moment. They pull away a little of each other in this scene of separation; Felix has discovered some of his manliness while Oscar has learned how to clean up the messes he creates. ❀

# List of Characters in
## *The Odd Couple*

**Oscar Madison** is a forty-three year old sports writer for the *New York Post*. Recently divorced from his wife Blanche, he lives in a pigsty that once was a lovely home befitting the upper eighties on Riverside Drive in New York City. Since his wife's departure, the place has been strewn with dirty dishes, disarrayed clothes and furniture, and other scattered debris. He hosts poker games every Friday night with his buddies, and he got through his divorce by drinking for four straight days and nights. When Felix, rejected by his wife, moves in, Oscar slowly cracks up over his friend's extreme fastidiousness. After Felix ruins a date for him, he finally demands that Felix move out. Yet after Felix leaves he realizes that his friend's penny-pinching, meticulous ways have influenced him positively. He has caught up on his alimony payments and begun to see the value of cleanliness.

**Felix Ungar**, a news writer, is one of Oscar's poker buddies. His extreme fastidiousness leads him to clean up after his maid, count his money obsessively, and cook meals with extraordinary care. The neurotic perfectionism that caused his wife to reject him begins to play itself out when he moves in with Oscar. He completely overhauls the apartment, making it immaculate and caring for it as if it were a museum. He spends poker nights serving drinks and sandwiches and cleaning ashtrays. When Oscar throws him out of the apartment, he finds new friends in the Pigeon sisters, and as a result of the altercation with Oscar and the compassion of the two sisters, he gains a new strength that allows him to stop pining after his wife and try to live with dignity.

**Speed** is one of Oscar's poker buddies. He is an irascible fellow, complaining and criticizing everyone. He is especially disgruntled by Felix's new regime of cleanliness in Oscar's apartment. When he leaves the poker game early, he accuses Oscar of bringing this new trouble upon himself by preventing Felix from committing suicide.

**Roy** is one of Oscar's poker buddies. His main complaint is the smoke in Oscar's apartment and the smell of the place.

**Vinnie** is one of Oscar's poker buddies. He is planning a trip to Florida in July, during the off-season. His rationale is that the hotel room will be much cheaper. Speed makes fun of him, predicting that his vacation will be "six cheap people in an empty hotel."

**Murray** is one of Oscar's poker buddies. His wife nags him so badly about not getting home too late that he constantly asks what time it is. A compassionate fellow, he worries about Felix when he does not show up for the poker game, and takes a sincere interest in his rehabilitation after the supposed suicide attempt. He adapts quickly to Felix's cleanliness regime, taking care not to spill crumbs on the table.

**The Pigeon sisters** are two bubbly, racy British sisters that live upstairs from Felix and Oscar. While initially full of laughs and bawdiness, the sisters are quickly brought to tears as Felix cries over his marital distress. Their suggestion to adjourn to their apartment strikes Oscar as a fortuitous turn of events while Felix's refusal to go serves as the breaking point for their relationship. ❀

# Critical Views on
## *The Odd Couple*

NORMAN NADEL ON THE PLAY'S LIVELINESS

[Norman Nadel is a theatre critic and the author of *A Pictorial History of the Theatre Guild* (1969). In this excerpt, Nadel commends the play's tremendous energy and self-sustaining comedy.]

You get the feeling that "The Odd Couple" doesn't even know it's in a theater—or is shrewd enough to keep such knowledge a secret. The Riverside Drive apartment setting on stage becomes a self-contained world, with the action charging along on some boisterous, inexhaustible life force of its own.

Inexhaustible life force could also apply to the playwright Neil Simon, director Mike Nichols and producer Saint Subber, who achieve a similar effect with last season's continuing comedy hit "Barefoot in the Park." "The Odd Couple" is at least as funny and far more substantial—the richest comedy Simon has written and purest gold for any theatergoer.

When you first encounter Oscar's apartment, during the regular Friday night poker game, it is so dirty you can almost smell it. The "buffet" he serves from his broken refrigerator consists of brown and green sandwiches, the green described as either very new cheese or very old meat.

This is the abode of an amiable slob, an impossible husband. Now divorced, he admits that when his wife asked him when he'd want dinner, he'd say he didn't know. Then wake her up at 3 A.M. and demand: "Now!"

The usually fastidious Matthau hulks through the role as if he'd never had a tidy impulse in his life. Disorder is something Oscar neither strives for nor resists; it is his own abiding presence, his atmosphere, his weather.

By contrast, his friend Felix (Carney) is obsessively neat, defiantly domestic and wildly emotional. Oscar describes him as the only man in the world with clenched hair. His marriage has just fallen apart for a number of reasons, of which one should suffice; he used to recook everything his wife had prepared.

So these two agree to share Oscar's eight dirty rooms, which seems like a practical idea until you examine it closely. That is just what playwright Simon has done, with hilarious findings.

The very characteristics which had demolished their respective marriages wreck living together for Oscar and Felix. The breakdown is more cataclysmic to them, being unexpected. The audience has seen how things are likely to go and gets the bonus of delicious anticipation.

There isn't a laggard scene in the whole play, though director Nichols' hand is more evident in those scenes which are well-peopled. The poker games—especially the opening one—are absolutely priceless. Nathaniel Frey, Paul Dooley, Sidney Armus and John Fiedler are the assisting aces in these.

Carole Shelley and Monica Evans portray the English sisters who live upstairs and come down for a dinner at home with Oscar and Felix. They enter late after six superlative actors have rocked the house with laughter, but they introduce a new, piquant note of comedy which the play is all ready for, at that point.

> —Norman Nadel, "Carney, Matthau Hilarious in Odd Couple," *The New York World-Telegram* (11 March 1965). In *New York Theatre Critics Reviews* (1965): p. 362.

## JOHN McCLAIN ON MARITAL ROLES IN THE PLAY

> [In this excerpt, McClain argues that the play's humor hinges on the spectacle of two men experiencing conflict in exactly the same terms as would a husband and wife.]

Mike Nichols seems to have the magic, and coupled with Neil Simon they present an unbeatable battery. Last season Mr. Simon wrote "Barefoot in the Park" and Mr. Nichols directed it and it is still hauling in the hay. Last night they unveiled their latest, "The Odd Couple," which will make nothing but more money.

This latest one is a sort of masculine love story. There is this fellow who is so impossibly meticulous, and such a frustrated housewife at heart, that his wife chases him into the street and he is rescued, on the verge of suicide, by his best friend.

Moving into his pal's apartment he makes life a nightmare of neatness and order. Between cooking, cleaning and crying—he succeeds finally in getting bounced by his benefactor. The story is that simple.

But with the combination of the author, who has a magnificent flair for the wild riposte, and the director, who can milk a silly scene until it squeals, this becomes a mad rigadoon which should really be a man-and-wife comedy but is instead the story of two guys, quite normal, who are utterly unable to live with one another.

It is a trick, really, but it works. Many of the funniest lines are exactly those that would be spoken by a husband and wife in the heat of a family argument, and while this situation wears thin after time there are the episodes, like the beginning of the third act, during which pantomime carries the comedy for the first several minutes.

There is a poker game comprised of an odd assortment of characters and two wonderfully gushing English girls who live in the same building to fill in the lapses in the proceedings, but the bulk of the evening is devoted to the antics of Walter Matthau, a divorced sports writer, and Art Carney, the chum he unhappily brings in to share his abode.

Mr. Matthau is a master of the slow burn and he employs this to excellent advantage; Mr. Carney, a skilled performer, is given a magnificent role as the male housekeeper. The final confrontation scene between the two is a masterpiece of performance and direction.

They get an abundance of help from the rest of the cast: Paul Dooley, Nathaniel Frey, Sidney Armus and John Fiedler as the card players, and Carole Shelley and Monica Evans as the two British gals.

Not that they need it, but Simon and Nichols have another socko success.

—John McClain, "A Socko Comedy Success," *New York Journal American* (11 March 1965). In *New York Theatre Critics Reviews* (1965): p. 364.

## HOWARD TAUBMAN ON NEIL SIMON'S WIDE APPEAL

[Howard Taubman, author of *The Making of American The-atre* (1965), wrote for *The New York Times* as a reporter, music critic, drama critic, and critic-at-large for forty two years. In this excerpt, Taubman remarks on Neil Simon's keen insight into opposing character types and his ability to dramatize this incongruity in a comic way.]

The opening scene in "The Odd Couple," of the boys in their regular Friday night poker game, is one of the funniest card sessions ever held on a stage.

If you are worried that there is nothing Neil Simon, the author, or Mike Nichols, his director, can think of to top that scene, relax. The main business of the new comedy, which opened last night at the Plymouth Theater, has scarcely begun, and Mr. Simon, Mr. Nichols and their excellent cast, headed by Art Carney and Walter Matthau, have scores of unexpected ways prepared to keep you smiling, chuckling and guffawing.

Mr. Simon has hit upon an idea that could occur to any play-wright. His odd couple are two men, one divorced and living in dejected and disheveled splendor in an eight-room apartment and the other about to be divorced and taken in as a roommate.

One could predict the course of this odd union from its formation in misery and compassion through its disagreements to its ultimate rupture. Mr. Simon's way of writing comedy is not to reach for gim-micks of plot; he probably doesn't mind your knowing the bare out-line of his idea.

His skill—and it is not only great but constantly growing—lies in his gift for the deliciously surprising line and attitude. His instinct for incongruity is faultless. It nearly always operates on a basis of character.

Begin with that poker game. Mr. Matthau, the slovenly host, is off stage in the kitchen fixing a snack while Nathaniel Frey, John Fiedler, Sidney Armus and Paul Dooley are sitting around the table on a hot summer night, sweating and grousing at the luck of the cards. The burly Mr. Frey is shuffling awkwardly, "for accuracy, not speed," and the querulous Mr. Fiedler, the big winner, talks of quitting early. ⟨. . .⟩

Mr. Matthau for his part is wonderfully comic as a man who finds his companion's fussy habits increasingly irksome. He walks about with a bearish crouch that grows more belligerent as his domestic situation becomes both familiar and oppressive. There is a marvelous scene in which he and Mr. Carney circle each other in mutual distaste—Mr. Matthau looking like an aroused animal about to spring and Mr. Carney resembling a paper tiger suddenly turned neurotic and dangerous.

To vary the humors of the domestic differences, Mr. Simon brings on two English sisters named Pigeon—yes Pigeon, Gwendolyn and Cecily—for a date with Oscar and Felix. The girls induce more laughter than their names promise. Carole Shelley and Monica Evans are a delight as the veddy British and dumb Pigeons.

Mr. Nichols's comic invention, like Mr. Simon's, shines through this production and the comfortable Riverside Drive apartment invoked by Oliver Smith's set. Just a sample: Mr. Carney left alone with the Pigeons is as nervous as a lad on his first date. When one of the girls takes out a cigarette, he hastens to her with his lighter and comes away with the cigarette clamped in its mechanism.

"The Odd Couple" has it made. Women are bound to adore the sight of a man carrying on like a little homemaker. Men are sure to snicker at a male in domestic bondage to a man. Kids will love it because it's funny. Homosexuals will enjoy it—for obvious reasons. Doesn't that take care of everyone?

—Howard Taubman, "Theater: Neil Simon's 'Odd Couple,'" *The New York Times* (11 March 1965). In *New York Theatre Critics Reviews* (1965): p. 363.

EDYTHE M. MCGOVERN ON THE PURSUIT OF HARMONY

[Edythe M. McGovern, author of *Neil Simon: A Critical Study* (1979) and *They're Never Too Young for Books: A Guide to Children's Books for Ages 1 to 8* (1994), is professor of English and Child Development at Los Angeles Valley

College. In this excerpt, McGovern argues that Simon's theme of polarized personalities is not gender-specific; rather, it serves as a template for any two people who cannot compromise.]

In this play Neil Simon has captured the essence of incompatibility among humans who repeat again and again their self-defeating patterns of personality, patterns which make it impossible for them to live together, all good intentions notwithstanding. It really does not matter that the two main characters, Oscar Madison and Felix Ungar (no connection to the unseen drama coach of the same name mentioned in *Come Blow Your Horn*), are both men. They could be women, or they could be a married couple in the traditional sense. What does matter is that the playwright is making a very humorous statement to the effect that although opposites may attract, they also exasperate, frequently to the point that the only viable alternative to murder is divorce. Even more noteworthy is the fact that the playwright has begun to allow his characters free rein in earnest, and he has been forced by them to do what amounts to an almost about-face in regard to sexual stereo-typing. ⟨. . .⟩

Neil Simon has publicly stated that many women have identified with Oscar and Felix and their situation, a fact which should not be surprising. As characters in *The Odd Couple* these two men are all too close to reality; they are not manipulated by the playwright, but actually represent scores of individuals of both sexes who can accomodate one another even in a long-lasting friendship, but who find it virtually impossible to parlay that friendship into an even closer relationship—marriage and the daily living which that entails. It is not that Felix is compulsively neat whereas Oscar is careless; it is not that Felix cries aloud while Oscar represses his feelings; it is not even that their total "chemistries" clash when they are forced to see each other on a daily basis. More significantly, neither man is able to compromise, particularly Felix, on even the smallest details of living. This kind of insensitivity to the need for mutual concession may be the genuine "grounds for divorce," rather than money or in-law trouble, statistics notwithstanding. Furthermore, what both men lack, and again, especially Felix, is a sense of humor, the variety which enables both men and women to see their own peculiarities and laugh, accepting themselves as parts played in the human comedy.

As always, Neil Simon's view is a benign one, tempered no doubt by his own warm and sympathetic attitude toward even the less attractive specimens of humanity. It is clear, however, that in this play he begins in earnest to deal in the comic genre with an ongoing and universal concern: the inevitable need for a middle course rather than an extremely polarized position in pursuit of harmony, if not ecstasy. And these two people would need to recognize this requirement were they both women or a heterosexual couple. In this sense, the playwright has significantly altered his previously held position regarding innate sexual differences, a position which he was probably quite unaware of having before creating *The Odd Couple.*

—Edythe M. McGovern, *Neil Simon: A Critical Study* (New York: Frederick Ungar Publishing Co., 1979): 46–47. Updated from her previous work, *Not-So-Simple Neil Simon* (Van Nuys, CA: Perivale, 1978): pp. 45–47.

RICHARD GRAYSON ON THE ABSENCE OF GAY
SUBTEXT IN THE PLAY

[Richard Grayson, whose nonfiction work has appeared in numerous periodicals including *Westerly Review* and *Madison Review,* is the author of several books of fiction including *With Hitler in New York and Other Stories* (1979) and *Eating at Arby's: The South Florida Stories* (1982). He has served as Visiting Assistant in Law at the Center for Governmental Responsibility at the University of Florida College of Law and Lecturer in American Literature at Nova Southeastern University. Exploring Simon's diverse approaches to the subject of homosexuality in his plays, Grayson in this excerpt argues that *The Odd Couple* contains no gay subtext.]

*The Odd Couple* (1965) is sometimes thought to have a gay subtext, but no cogent reading of the play can miss the fact that Oscar and Felix and their card-playing friends are blatantly heterosexual. Felix, despite being fussy and having a "feminine" interest in furniture and food, is strongly attracted to females. When he and his wife were happy, he still stared at women on the street "for ten minutes" and used to take the wrong subway home "just following a pair of legs." In addition, Oscar's threat to call Murray's wife and tell her that Murray was in Central Park wearing a dress would not get a laugh if the audience thought that the middle-aged policeman Murray was a transvestite or a homosexual. (As in *California Suite,* Simon here deliberately conflates cross-dressing and homosexuality.)

Much of what is funny about the relationship between Felix and Oscar in *The Odd Couple* is the incongruity of both tender feelings and spouse-like bickering between heterosexual men. If this relationship had any homoerotic overtones, the play would lose its humor. For example, when Felix gets a nerve spasm, saying that only his wife knows how to rub him so he can get relief, Oscar nevertheless succeeds in easing Felix's pain when he massages it; the comedy in the scene comes from the fact that it is one of the few times that one of them avoids rubbing the other the wrong way. Similarly, when Oscar suggests that Felix move in with him, he does it the way it is done between lovers: "I'm proposing to you. What do you want, a ring?" At the end of Act I, when Felix calls Oscar "Frances," his wife's name, the audience understands that it means only that Felix is settling into the same patterns in his (non-sexual) relationship with Oscar that led to the destruction of his marriage.

On the other hand, an oblique reference to the tenderness between homosexual lovers appears two decades later in *Broadway Bound* (1986), when Stan tells Eugene about a meeting with their estranged father, who had abandoned the family (much as Simon's own father had abandoned his). Stan and his father are having lunch, he reports, in Louie's Restaurant on Madison Avenue when his father asks whether Stan's mother, his ex-wife, is all right. Then the father starts to cry: "He grabbed my hand and held it. He sat there for half the lunch holding my hand. The waiter looked at us like we were a couple of lovers." That an emotional bond between father and son can be mistaken for homosexual affection in Simon's universe signifies the playwright's later understanding that gay men are not all that different.

—Richard Grayson, "The Fruit Brigade: Neil Simon's Gay Characters," *Neil Simon: A Casebook,* ed. Gary Konas (New York: Garland Publishing, Inc., 1997): pp. 137–147.

# Plot Summary of
## *Plaza Suite*

*Plaza Suite* is considered by many critics to be Neil Simon's transition from light comedies to more sensitive and probing material. It features three independent one-act plays that all take place in Suite #719 of the Plaza Hotel. In each playlet, Simon combines pathos with a modern comedy of manners, offering diverse but interwoven perspectives on the themes of love and marriage. In "Visitor from Mamaroneck," a twenty-four year marriage suffers from the husband's mid-life crisis, the wife's denial, and an opportunistic secretary; in "Visitor from Hollywood," a reunion of two former high school sweethearts becomes a showcase of emotional insecurities that are ultimately channeled into sex; and in "Visitors from Forest Hills," a married couple discovers they are inept at relieving their daughter's fear of matrimony on her wedding day. Simon's key characters are universally recognizable while also being individually unique. Their vulnerabilities are handled sensitively, yet they are also comically exaggerated. As in all his plays, Simon portrays his characters and their insecurities with combination of ridicule and affection.

Visitors from Mamaroneck

A bellhop escorts Karen Nash, described as "a pleasant affable woman who has let weight and age take their natural course," into Suite #719. She and her husband Sam will stay there for the night while their house is being painted; and coincidentally, it is the day of their 24th wedding anniversary. Karen laments to the bellhop that all of New York's oldest and most beautiful buildings are being torn down and replaced with new ones, thus foreshadowing her husband Sam's infidelity, which will later be revealed. Despite her resigned attitude, she decides to take advantage of this hotel stay to revitalize the marriage by ordering champagne, hors d'oeuvres, and flowers. After all, it is in room #719 that she and Sam spent their honeymoon 24 years ago.

When Sam arrives, it is clear that he cares more about his waistline, capped teeth, and meeting with his secretary about a contract that apparently cannot wait. When Karen mentions the anniversary, Sam can only point out to her that she has mistaken not only the date, but her own age. Obviously not interested in a romantic evening, Sam orders a spartan meal from room service. He becomes increasingly anxious in his wife's presence, and throughout this scene manages to negate every gesture she makes toward him. He is perturbed when Karen accidentally stabs him in the eyeball while helping him put in eyedrops. He is disappointed that Karen did not pack him any pajamas. Feeling trapped, he desperately wants a martini but is afraid it will make him flabby. Karen, who likes Sam flabby, reminds him this is the room in which they spent their honeymoon night; but Sam corrects her by saying they were one floor above. Sam buries himself in his work while Karen, bored and purposeless, looks on. She suggests a dirty movie, without success.

The waiter brings in the food, and Karen tells the waiter, much to Sam's chagrin, that it is their anniversary. Sam believes that he does not have to accept his age; he is 50 but feels he needn't be resigned to it. Karen, on the other hand, is perfectly comfortable with what the aging process has done to her face and figure, and feels no need to pretend she is a different age than she is. Jean McCormack, the secretary, arrives with supposedly urgent business for Sam, then informs him of computer trouble at the office. Sam takes the cue and explains that he must return to the office to clear up the problem before it gets out of hand. Karen, who finds out Jean is recently divorced, tells her it is their anniversary. Jean is surprised but not averted from the purpose of her amorous errand.

When Jean leaves, Karen asks Sam if he is having an affair, saying she understands if he needs to have an affair at this time in his life. Sam claims he wants to start the whole process of getting married, having kids and achieving success all over again; and he admits to having an affair with Jean. Sam offers to clear up the situation in whatever way Karen sees fit. Karen surmises, despite Sam's account of the affair, that the two have been seeing each other on the sly since his 50th birthday. Absolutely unwilling to make it easy on her husband, Karen gives Sam permission to have the affair so that he will be robbed of his guilt and martyrdom. Karen is disappointed in Sam's lack of originality. As Sam leaves, Karen tells Sam she will take Sam up on his offer to end the affair with his secretary. But Sam cannot do that—not tonight. He leaves, and room service arrives with the champagne Karen ordered for their anniversary.

Visitors from Hollywood

Jesse Kiplinger, a famous Hollywood producer staying in Suite #719, greets his anticipated visitor Muriel Tate, whom he has not seen in seventeen years. Muriel is now married with three kids and lives in New Jersey. Muriel, somewhat starstruck, is nervous around this old flame from her youth and calls him "Mr. Famous Hollywood Producer." She agrees to have a quick drink with him. Jesse does not need to fill Muriel in on what his life has been like; she has read in the newspapers about his Humphrey Bogart mansion in Beverly Hills and his star-filled life. Jesse, who calls Muriel the "last, sweet, simple, unchanged, unspoiled woman living in the world today," reveals that he has called her so that he can reassure himself that all women are not conniving and manipulative. He has been hurt badly by three gold-digging wives who "took the guts out of me" and longs for Muriel's simple honesty and frankness. Having let Jesse kiss her, Muriel becomes afraid and remorseful and prepares to leave. But Jesse tells her the sad story of his string of manipulative wives. Muriel insists that she is happy with her husband, but soon admits she suspects him of having an affair. Drunk by this time, Muriel kisses Jesse passionately. Though she insists she must go home, the lights go down as Jesse is unzipping her dress while naming all the stars he sat near at the Academy Awards.

Visitors from Forest Hills

It is Mimsey Hubley's wedding day, and she is locked in the bathroom of Suite #719 while her mother, Norma Hubley, waits anxiously for her. Mrs. Hubley is on the phone reassuring the impatient father of the groom. Yet, when her husband gets on the other end of the phone, she frantically insists he come upstairs immediately. Roy Hubley enters to find out that his daughter Mimsey has locked herself in the bathroom and refuses to come out and get married. Exasperated at the possibility of an enormous waste of money, Roy threatens Mimsey, ordering her to come out. Norma looks through the keyhole to find that Mimsey is crying. Roy hurls himself against the door, then realizes he may have broken his arm. He asks for a doctor.

Another phone call comes from Mr. Eisler, the father of the groom, whom Norma stalls by telling him to allow them just two more minutes. Norma is prepared to leave through the back door and move to Seattle out of sheer embarrassment if her daughter does not come out. Roy prepares to crawl out the ledge to the bathroom window, and Norma rips his coat trying to stop him. Even more exasperated, Roy goes out on the ledge. Once again, Norma must answer a call from Mr. Eisler and reassure him that all is running smoothly.

A heavy rain begins to fall. The doorbell rings, and Norma answers to find Roy in the doorway, having climbed in the window of a stranger's room while Mimsey, who locked the bathroom window, stood playing with her eyelashes. Norma's frustration reaches its peak as she bangs on the door and breaks her diamond ring. Roy gives up, saying he will go down to the Oak Room and drink to oblivion, yet Norma convinces him to take a kinder approach and persuade his daughter with love and understanding. Since Mimsey will not talk, but will respond to questions with two knocks for "yes" and one knock for "no", her parents are able to discern that she will allow only her father to enter the bathroom and talk with her. Norma is hurt that her daughter has chosen Roy. When Roy returns from the bathroom, having found out that Mimsey is afraid of building the kind of married life she sees her parents living, he calls Borden, the groom, up to the room. Borden very simply shouts "cool it!" through the bathroom door and then leaves, saying "see you downstairs."

Mimsey then emerges from the bathroom and takes her father's arm; amidst Roy's indignant complaints about the crassness of his son-in-law to be, the three make their way out of the hotel room and down to the wedding. ❁

# List of Characters in
## *Plaza Suite*

Visitors from Mamaroneck

**Karen Nash** is the wife of Sam. She is forty-eight years old and "makes no bones about it." She is described as "a pleasant, affable woman who has let weight and age take their natural course." She is quite aware that her husband is having an affair, but spends most of the scene pretending that she doesn't care. When Sam admits to the affair, she asks him to stop seeing Miss McCormack and work it out with her. Karen's nonchalant attitude toward the affair proves to be just an act.

**Sam Nash** is fifty years old but cannot accept it and tries to hide his age. "Everything about Sam," Simon indicates, "is measured, efficient, economic." He has been having an affair with his secretary in an effort to rejuvenate his life and defy the aging process, but instead of loosening him up, it seems to have made him even more disturbed. When pressured, Sam admits to having an affair with Miss McCormack. Seeming tortured by Karen's knowledge of his affair, he leaves the hotel room in search of his mistress.

**Jean McCormack** is Sam's secretary. She is "a trim, attractive woman about twenty-eight . . . neatly dressed, bright, cheerful, and smilingly efficient." She has been recently divorced. She speaks in code to Sam in front of Karen in order to conceal their plans for a tryst.

Visitors from Hollywood

**Jesse Kiplinger**, described as a forty-year-old "confident, self-assured man" dressed in "Hollywood mod," is a successful Hollywood producer who is visiting in New York to sign John Huston for his next picture. A victim of three gold-digging wives, he longs for Muriel's simplicity and naivete. He is delighted to find that she still possesses these qualities, and seduces her.

**Muriel Tate** lives in Tenafly, New Jersey with her husband and three children. She has never left the suburbs and seems to have retained some of the naivete associated with them. When Jesse begins to flirt with her, she cites her happy family as a reason to stay away from him. But as she gets more and more drunk, she reveals her suspicion that her husband is having an affair. Drunk on vodka and Jesse's celebrity, she goes to bed with him.


Visitors from Forest Hills

**Norma Hubley** is the mother of the bride. She is extremely nervous about her daughter's reluctance to get married on her wedding day. Her fear of committing a social faux pas is so great that she vows she will leave the hotel out the back door and move to Seattle if her daughter calls off the wedding. When her daughter finally agrees to talk to her father, Norma is hurt that Mimsey did not choose to talk to her.

**Roy Hubley** is the father of the bride. His daughter's behavior incenses him; he is worried about the enormous expense that will be lost if she refuses to marry. Neither is he pleased with his wife, whom he believes should have been able to persuade her daughter to come out of the bathroom. Though Mimsey chooses to speak to him, he is baffled and insulted that her fiancé Borden barked "cool it" to Mimsey. Roy is both aggravated by Borden's crass speech and envious of his persuasive powers.

**Mimsey Hubley** is a bride to be who has locked herself in the bathroom of her bridal suite on the day of her wedding. When she finally grants her father access to the bathroom, she tells him that she is afraid her married life will be like her parents'. The Hubleys surmise that the fighting and bickering are what scare their daughter. Her fiancé Borden's order to "cool it" changes her mind, and she comes out of the bathroom ready to be married.

**Borden Eisler** is the groom. When he finds that Mimsey is having second thoughts about marrying him, he simply marches up to her room and, through the bathroom door, tells her to "cool it." It is clear that he knows Mimsey better than her parents do, and when Mimsey comes out of the bathroom, the Hubley's are both amazed and jealous. ❀

# Critical Views on
## *Plaza Suite*

CLIVE BARNES ON GEORGE C. SCOTT'S AND MAUREEN
STAPLETON'S PERFORMANCES

[Clive Barnes, author of many books including *Inside American Ballet Theatre* (1983) and editor of *Best American Plays*
(Seventh and Eighth Series 1975, 1983) has contributed
music, drama, dance and film reviews to *Daily Express*
(London), *The Spectator* (London), *The New York Times* and
*The New York Post*. In this excerpt, Barnes evaluates the performances of the two lead actors as extensions of Simon's
machinelike comic talent.]

Neil Simon clearly believes a play is a machine for laughing at, and
"Plaza Suite," which opened at the Plymouth Theater last night,
evokes laughter in plenty. Made up of three one-act farces, the
evening, after a slow start with the first, warms up with the second
and ends with an all-stops-out, grandstand finish with the third.

This ending is hilarious, as funny a contrivance as Mr. Simon
and his demon director, Mike Nichols, have ever offered us in the
theater. In essence it is little more than a revue sketch, yet its pace,
style and manner give it something of the well-groomed elegance
of a Feydeau farce.

It is a wedding reception. Downstairs at the Plaza the guests have
gathered and are busy eating hors d'oeuvres, drinking the drinks and
waiting for the bride. Upstairs, in the Plaza suite that is the hero of
the evening, the bride's parents are also waiting for the bride. But
they are chewing fingernails rather than hors d'oeuvres, for the bride
has locked herself in the bathroom and will not come out. Disgrace
is imminent, and the parents, George C. Scott and Maureen Stapleton, fight valiantly to avert it.

Mr. Simon is extraordinarily adept at building up, just like a house
of cards, an initially flimsy situation, and here with the bride's parents locked out, bullying, cajoling, pleading and most of all sweating,
the playlet has all the momentum derived from the inevitable
progress of the inevitable.

Mr. Scott, smiling like a bloodstained shark and croaking like a gangster sealion, is marvelous as the father who counts up the wedding expenses with the paternal click of a cash-register mind, and is determined not to let anything stand in the way between his daughter and a fully paid-up altar, not even a bathroom door.

Equally as fine is Miss Stapleton, looking rather like a crumpled cabbage with courage and fighting back against a day that is already the worst in her life and is rapidly deteriorating. She ladders her stocking. She thinks her husband has dropped seven elegant Plaza stories down to become a Hawaiian punch outside Trader Vic's. And then it starts to rain.

Mr. Nichols' method is superbly physical. To disclose his visual gags would be as unfair as stealing Mr. Simon's wisecracks, but one moment where, with the speed of a stealthy black mamba striking, Mr. Scott picks up a chair, darts across the bed, aims the chair at the door, thinks better of it, and subsides to the other side of the room, is masterly. And best of all the whole sequence is conceived and executed in one arc of movement.

Almost as hilarious as this reluctant walk up the bridal path is the second playlet where an aging Hollywood producer, with a cashmere sweater and a head with a fringe on top, seduces his boyhood girl-friend who, despite an unfortunate taste for vodka stingers, has never left the suburbs.

The now middle-aged girl-friend has watched the producer from afar, vicariously glorying in his success, and is now only too respectably eager to literally waltz into the bedroom to the well-spun tales of Hollywood fan gossip. It is silly, but funny, and for all its exaggeration it is the only one of the sketches that has much relationship to life—it is almost beyond farce, almost close to comedy.

Miss Stapleton, whose slightly tipsy sparrow anxiety has an undertone of love to it, and Mr. Scott, with his rapacious, smoothly routined seduction course—doors unobtrusively locked, hands wandering with a subtle boldness and a voice efficiently pleading like a little lost boy come home—play together with the certainty of swordsmen, although they are playing in a rather different style.

Miss Stapleton acts to the audience, Mr. Scott acts to himself. Indeed most of the time throughout his consciously virtuoso performance there seem to be two George C. Scotts, one acting and one standing outside admiringly to lead the applause. It doesn't matter—in this kind of play it rather adds to the fun.

Mr. Simon—at least in "Plaza Suite"—is at his worst when at his most serious. His first playlet of a suburban marriage wryly on the rocks reveals the limitations of heartless, machine-made humor. Wisecracks are scattered throughout the dialogue like machine-gun fire, but do nothing to show any genuine insight into a marriage falling apart after 23 or 24 years, despite Miss Stapleton's gallant attempt to make the wife vulnerably believable and Mr. Scott's bear-like gruffness as the husband who refuses to age.

Clearly, then, Mr. Simon is at his best doing what comes naturally to him, clanking his old laughter machine and getting his jokes as reliably as the messages in fortune cookies. And it takes no message in a fortune cookie to be assured that in "Plaza Suite" the old team of Simon and Nichols has done it again, and will once more set the town laughing.

—Clive Barnes, "Theater: 'Plaza Suite,' Neil Simon's Laugh Machine," *The New York Times* (15 February 1968). In *New York Theatre Critics Reviews* (1968): p. 348.

WALTER KERR ON BALANCING SERIOUSNESS WITH GAGS

[Walter Kerr (1913–1996), author of *How Not to Write a Play, The Decline of Pleasure,* and *The Silent Clowns,* won the Pulitzer Prize for drama criticism in 1978 for his work at *The New York Times.* In this excerpt, Kerr admires Simon's ability to inject the appropriate amount of seriousness into his comedy.]

I admire "Plaza Suite" very much, and not for the most obvious reason. The obvious reason for tipping one's hat to it is that this sort of apparently idle, always amiable, cork-popping improvisation is exceedingly difficult to bring off; if it weren't, we'd have hordes of such "trifles" instead of one good one every two years. Mr. Simon, unlike most of the hopefuls who save up quips until they've got 120 pages of them ready to be typed, knows precisely what he is doing. But there's a better reason for saluting him than that. What he is doing is precisely right—for him and for the form he works in. ⟨. . .⟩

One of the crazy mistakes we make in the contemporary theater is that of supposing that if something is serious at all it must be thoroughly, thumpingly serious—and must promptly be put into a bigger, deeper, soberer play. That is how we get our overinflated dramas in which almost nothing happens, certainly nothing ample enough to account for all of the soul-scratching, conscience-prodding, emotion-begging writhing that goes on. The play becomes overwrought because it is making too much of a small truth. There *are* small truths, and they are comic truths, they are truths of a size that can be accommodated in—and almost cheerfully covered over by— a quip. We quip them into statement, and then into silence, every day of our lives. Feeling 50, and having energy that can never be properly used again, is one of them. Being bowled over by celebrities, especially if we have come within inches of brushing lives with them, is another. They are legion, they are not tragic (they are too ordinary for that and we are all helpless in their damnable hands), they are shrug-off truths, silly imprisonments and hopeless reflexes that can only be dealt with by pretending to laugh. By actually laughing, finally, more or less as George Scott laughs, with desperate exuberance. The highest home of such truths is the epigram—which is, of all things, a one-liner. But there are some so commonplace that a wisecrack will take care of them, and thank God for that. If all men are trapped, some have the sense to see that they are trapped in a circus ring.

Mr. Simon seems to me a man of sense, using just the jigger and a half of substance that will make a decent drink, observing what he observes and cradling it in a joke that is about the right fit for it. His work is not only smooth and sunny, it is nicely proportioned— which is more than can be said for that of many of his perspiring fellows. He has no identity problem.

—Walter Kerr, "Simon's Funny—Don't Laugh," *The New York Times* (15 February 1968). In *New York Theatre Critics Reviews* (1968): p. 347.

MARTIN GOTTFRIED ON SIMON'S CYNICISM

[Martin Gottfried, author of numerous books including *A Theater Divided: The Postwar American Stage* (1967) and *All His Jazz: The Life & Death of Bob Fosse* (1990) has contributed drama and music reviews to *Women's Wear Daily, Village Voice, The New York Post, The New York Times Magazine, Newsweek,* and others. In this excerpt, Gottfried argues that Simon's pointed, wisecrack humor falls short of his usual genius for nonsensical comedy.]

I wouldn't call them one-act plays—they're barely sketches and are more nearly vaudeville routines, which is pretty much the way Mike Nichols directed them—but whatever they are, and despite whatever equivocation is about to follow, Neil Simon's three pieces that make up "Plaza Suite" (last night at the Plymouth Theatre) are very, very funny and don't forget that. Comedy—not comedy intended but comedy funny—is not something you run across every day or for that matter, every season.

The common theme is marriage, a recurring Simon concern, and the attitude toward it is dismal, also a recurring Simon theme. The common locale is a room at the Plaza Hotel. In the first play ("Visitor From Mamaroneck") a couple is celebrating a 23rd anniversary and I had to check my notes to recall the basic story. Mind you, it is now only fifteen minutes since I left the theatre. That is how substantial this entertainment is.

In any case, the two are apparently settled and comfortable, the wife vaguely trying to recapture romance and the husband interested only in his business. It is not very long before we realize that he is having an affair, although Simon takes practically the play's length to reveal it. It is difficult to believe that after he introduces us to the husband's secretary he still thinks we are suspecting nothing. Or perhaps he figured that it made no difference. The point (that husbands will become restless) is too trivial to bother about and if it weren't for Maureen Stapleton's uncanny depth there would be no serious feeling to the thing at all.

But the truth is that Simon would rather be funny than serious and if there is any crucial problem with "Plaza Suite" it is that he occasionally thinks that the humor is pointed. As a result, and unlike some of his better comic writing, "Plaza Suite" is completely restricted to wise-crack comedy rather than the nonsense humor that is actually Simon's genius.

In any case, this first piece is regularly amusing without really breaking you up. Scott is fairly stiff but then the character he is playing is stiff. Working as straight man (and performing all the duties such a role demands) he lets Miss Stapleton lay on the jokes and she does it beautifully, proving for the first time to me that an Actors Studio-trained actor can play comedy.

The second piece ("Visitor From Hollywood") is the least effective of the evening, though it is not unfunny. A successful Hollywood producer summons a New Jersey girl-friend of 17 years ago, looking for a little action. She is thrilled, having followed his career through all the gossip columns and filled with visions of Hollywood-star stories. The best part of this is that he believes all the stories himself and is no less movie-magazine-mad than she.

This is basically a seduction routine and it is neither original nor especially funny until its conclusion, which is a bedroom scene drenched in gorgeously cascading dropped names. Scott's work is neatly straight-faced though his mugging tends to get out of hand and Nichols is to be blamed for that. Miss Stapleton, wonderfully made up to look like a housewife trying to seem girlish, is again delightful although she was unable to make much of the dissatisfying marriage that has led up to the hotel-room visit.

The final piece ("Visitor From Forest Hills") is by far the funniest, and Simon builds a continuous stream of jokes into a barrage of comedy. A man is spending $8,000 on his daughter's wedding and the girl has locked herself in the bathroom, refusing to come out. Much of the humor is based on the father's concern for the expense and it tends to get repetitious, but the whole business of prying the girl out is turned into near-slapstick and Simon has never been funnier (though he has been more clever). Here, Scott is absolutely splendid, desperately holding onto his dignity while it shreds like his "rented ripped coat" (saying "rented ripped coat" rather than "ripped rented coat" is exactly the dry Simon humor that is absent from these plays).

Nichols' direction throughout is gorgeously confident and it is impossible to tell where he begins and Simon leaves off. Both are being ultra-professional but both are not doing their best stuff. That leaves "Plaza Suite" as condescending in a way and perhaps even cynical. But it is still genuine entertainment and there's no sense denying that.

—Martin Gottfried, "Plaza Suite," *Women's Wear Daily* (15 February 1968). In *New York Theatre Critics Reviews* (1968): p. 349.

RICHARD P. COOKE ON THE EXPERTISE OF NEIL SIMON AND MIKE NICHOLS

[Richard P. Cooke covered aviation and theatre for *The Wall Street Journal* for thirty years, and retired from his position there as Broadway and Off Broadway Drama Critic in 1969. In this excerpt, Cooke points to the effective moments in each of the three sketches.]

Neil Simon and Mike Nichols make it easy for a reviewer. Their new Broadway entertainment, "Plaza Suite," produced by Saint-Subber at the Plymouth Theater, is not one play but three, and all of them are very funny and everyone in his right mind should go and see them, and that's that. It has been said that no one knows where lightning will strike, but the Simon-Nichols combination, which has turned out such delights as "Barefoot in the Park" and "The Odd Couple," constitutes one of the best theatrical lightning rods around.

Lest all the credit go to writer and director, though, it must be said that George C. Scott and Maureen Stapleton, usually associated with more weighty drama, are marvelous. Mr. Scott uncovers a great flair for farce and Miss Stapleton, about as far as possible from her characterization in "The Rose Tattoo," here plays a succession of suburban matrons with stimulating gusto. She is a warm rather than a brittle comedienne, which is all to the good.

The action of all three playlets takes place in suite 719 of the Plaza Hotel, which must be on the northeast corner because the occupants claim they can see both the new General Motors Building and Central Park (one of them is afraid the Park is going to be torn down and replaced with a supermarket). All three are also commentaries on marriage in one way or another. Nothing much funnier than a comedy about marriage or the lack of it has turned up lately, and Mr. Simon has uncovered some new veins in this vast orebody.

The first play is entitled "A Visitor from Mamaroneck," that suburban town in Westchester County often used synonymously with White Plains or Scarsdale as a seat of conventionality. Enter one Karen Nash (Miss Stapleton), a lady nearing 50 and flushed with the memories of her honeymoon in this very suite 27 years before. Champagne is ordered and all is set for a second, or perhaps 27th, honeymoon, when in comes businessman husband Sam (Mr. Scott). Thence develops one of those contests between the romantic practicality of womankind and the impractical romance of men.

There is nothing much in the play but the abrasion, always kept at the laughing point, of personalities. Toward the end, Sam's secretary comes in and before the curtain is down he has admitted to an affair with her, resisted the pleadings of Karen for a reconciliation and gone out to his office rendezvous. But Mr. Simon lets some warmth slip in with the rather pathetic figure of Karen.

Mr. Scott is next discovered in informal garb, his somewhat harsh and determined features topped by a blondish wig that makes him look like a dissipated Hotspur relaxing after battle. Here he is a successful Hollywood producer about to entertain a girl he knew in high school days in the East. She is now a matron, with a fresh makeup and a white band across her dark, smoothly brushed hair, and is played by Miss Stapleton.

What follows in "A Visitor From Hollywood" proves the art of seduction can be made very funny. Miss Stapleton's Muriel is forever talking about how happily married she is and how she and her husband get along and pretending she must get her hat and gloves on and be off to do her shopping. But when asked about a drink, she calls for a vodka stinger, and moves ever toward the Big Event, the most willing of unwilling victims.

The last of the three is called "Visitor From Forest Hills." The situation might seem too slight even for a one-acter, but if Mr. Simon had extracted any more laughter out of it with farce and sight gags, the health of some of the onlookers might have been endangered.

All that happens is that a bride in Room 719 locks herself in the bathroom as the groom, the guests and that expensive orchestra and buffet, wait in vain below. No one probably would believe it, but a conversation with a bathroom door proves to have a great deal of merit. First practiced by Miss Stapleton as the mother, all gussied up in a flowery hat and glittering gown for the wedding, it proves a fruitless plea. Soon joined by Mr. Scott as the father of the bride, the assault upon the non-speaking daughter rises to battlefield intensity. It is a great ploy.

Mr. Scott, resembling a cross between Andrew Jackson and George Romney, rolls his eyes frightfully under his disarrayed gray wig and suffers all manner of indignities before the daughter emerges because of an entirely different type of urging—a word from her own generation.

"Plaza Suite" should be around as long as Miss Stapleton and Mr. Scott feel they can stand the pace, and they both look pretty durable.

—Richard P. Cooke, "Simon and Nichols Again," *The Wall Street Journal* (16 February 1968). In *New York Theatre Critics Reviews* (1968): pp. 349–350.

## WILLIAM GOLDMAN ON SIMON'S SUNNY WRITING

[William Goldman, author of numerous books of fiction and nonfiction, including *Tinsel* (1979) and *Hype and Glory* (1990), received two Academy Awards for *Butch Cassidy and the Sundance Kid* (best original screenplay 1970) and *All the President's Men* (best screenplay adaptation 1976). In this excerpt, Goldman argues that "Visitor from Mamaroneck" represents a tentative step away from his usual "sunny" perspective toward "the dark side."]

*Plaza Suite* was originally four short plays, all occurring in the same suite at the Plaza Hotel. The first, virtually a monologue for George C. Scott, the male star, was cut during rehearsal, not because it wasn't funny—it may have been the funniest of the four—but because it didn't fit with the rest of the show, which didn't need any more laughs as it was and was also running long.

⟨. . .⟩ "Mamaroneck," the longest of the trio, is not only the best of the three and the best thing Simon has yet written, it is also, I think, the watershed play of his career.

For me, Simon is the most skillful playwright to have surfaced in the sixties. Not the best. The most skillful. What keeps him from being the best is that with all his skill he is trivial: you don't even remember what *Barefoot in the Park* was about when you're applauding the curtain calls. He is almost afraid to let a moment pass without laughter. A friend of his says: "Doc's never really relaxed unless a joke has just paid off or he's got one building." But friends also say that in real life he isn't like that; it isn't always happy-ending time with lots of laughs before the fade-out clinch. He is a bright man with a good mind and a fine supply of bile.

Only he can't quite tap it yet.

"Mamaroneck," for example, was originally going to be a full-length play, and the version that is playing now was the first act. "But after I finished what I've got now, I thought, 'That's really the end of it.' I couldn't think of an ending. In order to go on with it I would have had to write a happy ending: the second act would have shown him living with this young girl, maybe, and the third act would just be getting together again with his wife."

But aren't there other possibilities? Scott could have been happy living with the young girl; or Stapleton could have ended up happy, to her own surprise, now that she was done with a rotten marriage; or Scott could have been happy living with the young girl, but the young girl might have found him too old for her, too predictable, too dull. There are any number of other possibilities, all of them conceivable, all of them valid.

All of them a little on the dark side.

But Simon writes sunny. That, I think, is the main reason why he is so beyond-words successful; there is a sunny quality to his work, and you feel good when it's over. Not smarter; not cleansed; just good. And even though his thoughts are filled with shadows, his writing landscape is always bright. Now this would be fine, if he saw the world that way, but he doesn't. In other words, the fact that he says he would have had to *write* a happy ending is true, but he doesn't *feel* that a happy ending would ever have happened. He says: "I don't think the guy ever comes back to his wife. So many people around fifty have left their wives and married their secretaries; it's sort of a horrible thing."

But the "horrible thing" is more than he can put down now. That's why I think "Mamaroneck" is so crucial to his development; the man can go on doing "entertainment pieces" till the world looks level. The question is, will he? Or will he continue in the same direction as the first tentative step taken in "Mamaroneck"? God knows it is tentative; it was all he could do to end the play enigmatically, without some kind of contrived happy ending.

—William Goldman, *The Season: A Candid Look at Broadway* (New York: Harcourt, Brace & World, Inc., 1969): pp. 319, 320–321.

EDYTHE M. MCGOVERN ON CHARACTER VERISIMILITUDE

[Edythe M. McGovern, author of *Neil Simon: A Critical Study* (1979) and *They're Never Too Young for Books: A Guide to Children's Books for Ages 1 to 8* (1994), is professor of English and Child Development at Los Angeles Valley College. In this excerpt, McGovern shows that the subtle differences between the characters from sketch to sketch lend them a verisimilitude that offsets their caricatured qualities.]

Under the title *Plaza Suite* Neil Simon has written three short plays, unified by the use of Suite 719 in New York's Plaza Hotel as the setting common to all. In professional productions the main characters are played by the same two players, a device which is undoubtedly a source of delight for versatile performers, since the people portrayed are a different couple in each play. As the visitors come to 719, they undergo crisis-type situations, although the plays are certainly comedies if audience laughter is any yardstick. The plots are simple, and the sparkling dialogue, preposterous situations, and even farcical behavior are typical of Simon's work. However, beneath the banter and even the "shtick" we are invited to consider some matters of great seriousness, such as aging in American society, marital infidelity, the emptiness of success, non-communication, and the generation gap.

These are comedies, but in the first play we are not given the traditional happy ending, and in the other two playlets there are serious questions raised which are left unanswered. Several of the characters are somewhat exaggerated, but they remain believable because each one's behavior is "logical" for him or her, as conceived by the playwright.

There is an interesting commonality among the three principal male characters: Sam Nash, Jesse Kiplinger, and Roy Hubley. Each man has achieved the visible trappings of success as our middle-class world views that phenomenon. Each has reached the forty to fifty age bracket and somehow discovered that "winning the goal" does not necessarily bring the satisfactions associated with that feat. Sam and Jesse are determined to remain young through extra-marital sexual activity, and we feel that given the opportunity, Roy Hubley would do exactly the same thing. The wives, two of whom are also middle-aged, have "settled" with life, at least until we look at them closely. The young bride-to-be in "Forest Hills" is so afraid of becoming like her mother that she almost misses getting married at all, and the "other woman" in "Mamaroneck" is almost a stereotype of a young divorcée who has resumed her maiden name and skips dinners to maintain her slim figure. She is the efficient secretary who doubles as the boss's mistress because that is the way *she* wants it.

There are young people and children in these families although the only ones we see onstage appear in "Forest Hills." Somehow they seem disappointing to their parents, although they are also very much loved and perhaps a bit pampered. ⟨. . .⟩

In *Plaza Suite* the characters are memorable because, with the possible exception of Jean McCormack, they are unique individuals, still retaining a universality by representing an entire group of people. If Sam Nash, Jesse Kiplinger, and Roy Hubley share some problems, as noted earlier, this does not mean that the playwright merely presents cardboard images of three prosperous men who find middle-age disappointing. It is evident that the Nashes are more sophisticated than the Hubleys. It is clear that succeeding as a Hollywood producer is quite different from succeeding as a New York business man. Therefore, it is logical that Sam Nash can verbalize more easily than Roy Hubley, and that Jesse Kiplinger is the most articulate of the three men, as well as the phoniest.

If we examine the three wives, we see that only Norma Hubley has gone the whole way in playing the role of conventional wife-mother. She and Roy are not really happy, but "that's the way it goes." Karen Nash would gladly accept the same role, but she has enough insight to understand that her life is not working well and to be concerned about it. She is willing to do anything to keep Sam. Muriel Tate is still in her thirties, but she has already discovered that doing what society in Tenafly expects a wife-and-mother-of-three to do is not satisfying. So she lives in an unrealistic world, colored by vodka stingers. At any rate, all of these characters have enough verisimilitude, in spite of some exaggeration for the sake of comedy, to function as conduits through which the playwright's serious themes flow.

—Edythe M. McGovern, *Neil Simon: A Critical Study* (New York: Frederick Ungar Publishing Co., 1979): pp. 58–9, 69–70. Updated from her previous work, *Not-So-Simple Neil Simon* (Van Nuys, CA: Perivale, 1978).

# Plot Summary of
## *The Sunshine Boys*

Neil Simon's *The Sunshine Boys* revives the vaudevillian comic tradition. A type of theatrical entertainment that was popular in the United States during the late nineteenth and early twentieth centuries, vaudeville reached its peak of popularity in the late 1920s. Its leading venue was the Palace Theater in New York City, and star performers included Eddie Cantor, Burns and Allen, W. C. Fields, and Buster Keaton. A vaudeville show typically included a series of acts such as juggling, songs, dramatic sketches, dances, acrobatics, and comedy skits like the one performed by Willie Clark and Al Lewis in this play. Vaudeville, much like Simon's aged characters, became practically obsolete with the arrival of radio and motion pictures. Willie and Al, known as the famous "Lewis and Clark" in their prime, are fictionalized versions of the famous vaudeville duo Joe Smith and Charles Dale.

Neil Simon pays tribute to vaudeville with both the content and the form of his play. His aged characters are brimming with memories of the good old days, and their skit, though executed poorly, is a nostalgic memento of a lost comedic form. In addition, Simon structures and times the dialogue to give the entire play the feel of a vaudeville sketch. As the critic Robert K. Johnson explains, "He not only includes a wacky vaudeville skit within *The Sunshine Boys*, but deftly integrates this skit's speech patterns and point of view in all the scenes preceding and following the skit" (*Neil Simon* 139). In this sense, Simon's play envelopes the audience in a time and an art form long past.

**Act One, Scene One** takes place in Willie Clark's hotel room, which is described as "rather a depressing place." It is mid winter and Willie, a former vaudeville star who has passed his prime, lives out his day like all the others, watching TV and dozing off. He is absent minded and clumsy, kicking out the TV plug accidentally and calling the repair service to blame it on them. Ben Silverman, Willie's nephew and agent, arrives at the door and must coach the confused Willie on how to slide the latch to let him in. This is his regular Wednesday visit, and as always Ben brings his uncle a copy of *Variety* and some cigars. Willie pesters Ben to get him an audition, believing he is only a step away from getting a part in a musical or some other show. He reminisces about his six appearances on the *Ed Sullivan Show* and the good old days of vaudeville. Ben reminds Willie of the fiascos that occurred the last time he got him auditions for commercials: Willie could never remember his lines.

Today's visit, however, is different. The Vice President of CBS, a longtime fan of Willie's, wants Willie and his old comedy partner Al Lewis (the famed Lewis and Clark, or the "Sunshine Boys") to perform in a televised variety show tracing the history of comedy. Willie is adamant against it because he has been harboring resentment at his partner Al for twelve years. Though Al was the best in the business, he tortured Willie by poking him in the chest and spitting on him when he pronounced his "t"s. Al's worst offense was retiring suddenly without consulting Willie; in effect, he retired both of them. Ben manages to persuade Willie to meet with Al, but Willie threatens to sue if Al pokes or spits.

The following Monday is the day Al and Willie will meet for the first time in twelve years (**Scene Two**). When Al arrives at Willie's room, the two begin to bicker and criticize each other. Both men carefully protect their pride, both from each other and from the industry that has passed them by. Both agree to do the variety show, not because they want to, but as a favor to their families. They agree to rehearse their famous sketch "The Doctor Will See You Now." Demonstrating their talent for playing off each other despite themselves, they wrangle over the arrangement of their set and the wording of a minor line. As tempers escalate, Al pokes Willie in the chest and Willie threatens him with a knife. A phone call from Al's daughter breaks up the fight. She convinces them to give each other another chance, but upon resuming their rehearsal they immediately return to the same angry stalemate. Neither will compromise, and each insists he is right.

**Act Two, Scene Two** takes place on the set of the TV station. It has been made up as doctor's office. Lewis and Clark, who have resolved their differences enough to make it to the set, have held up the taping session with their quibbling over minor details like the length of the tongue depressor. They finally begin the sketch, which is a classic vaudeville farce filled with witty one-liners and physical comedy. Simon bases this sketch on the actual "Dr. Krankheit and His Only Living Patient," which was performed by Joe Smith and

Charlie Dale. All goes well for a while, but Willie breaks character when Al spits in his face, and again when Al pokes Willie's chest. As Willie's anger intensifies, he clutches his chest and falls to the floor. The scene ends as the announcer records a revised introduction to the *Sunshine Boys:* they will show a clip from the *Ed Sullivan Show* 11 years ago.

**Act Two, Scene Two** finds Willie back in his hotel room, this time with a registered nurse. During the ensuing conversation between Willie and the nurse, it becomes clear that Simon has made these two ornery characters the unwitting practitioners of more farcical humor. The nurse has no tolerance for Willie's temperamental outbursts; she fires his abuse right back at him. When Ben arrives, he tells Willie that due to his heart attack he must retire. He gives him the choice of moving in with him and his family or moving to the Actors' Home in New Brunswick. When Willie asks if Ben will visit him in the home, Ben realizes that this is the first time Willie has treated him like a nephew and not an agent. Willie has let him get a little closer. Willie agrees to see Al, who is waiting downstairs, because he thinks he might get an apology out of him. But when Al arrives, it is clear he will not. Al tells Willie that his troubles were self-inflicted.

Al announces that he will be moving to the Actors' Home in New Brunswick. Without telling Al that he will also be there, Willie indicates that they will see each other again. Out of what seems like sheer fatigue, the two begin to soften toward each other and let go of their anger. Before long, they are reminiscing about the past like old friends.

The end of this play brings to focus a theme that has been prevalent in this play: the sad but hilarious foibles of old age. Willie's and Al's old age makes them laughably stubborn and insecure, but it also represents their nearness to death, a fact that is suddenly foregrounded when Willie suffers a heart attack. For Willie and Al, comedy has always been serious: it has made them a living, and now it staves off death. Humor serves Willie and Al as well as it serves the playwright: it makes the idea of aging approachable, and ultimately it fosters compassion, warmth, and respect for individuals who by the world's standards have become obsolete. ❀

# List of Characters in
## *The Sunshine Boys*

**Willie Clark** is a former vaudeville star, one half of the Lewis and Clark (aka "Sunshine Boys") team. In his old age he has become forgetful, clumsy, and extremely stubborn. He lives for the possibility of getting a part in a musical or television show, and his week revolves around getting *Variety* and keeping up on the fate of old stars like himself. He has held a grudge against his former partner Al Lewis for many years, but eventually lets it go after suffering a heart attack brought on by a fight with him.

**Ben Silverman** is Willie's nephew and agent. He serves as Willie's primary caretaker, checking on him once a week and putting up with his irascibility as much as he can. His weekly visits give him chest pains, and he makes sure Willie is aware of that. After Willie's heart attack and forced retirement, Ben notices gratefully that his uncle finally treats him like a nephew and not an agent.

**Al Lewis** is a former vaudeville performer and comedy partner to Willie Clark. He has a penchant for poking his partner in the chest and spitting when he pronounces "t"s, but Willie cannot deny that in his day he was known as a master of comic timing and execution. Eleven years ago, after a less than perfect performance on the *Ed Sullivan Show*, Al told Willie he was retiring. Since then, Willie has not been able to forgive him for calling off the act before he was ready.

**Eddie** is the assistant director for the television studio in which Willie and Al tape their sketch. He is described as wearing a "headset and speaker, trailing wires and carrying a clipboard." He helps the director by mediating between the idiosyncratic demands of the actors and the furious impatience of the director.

**Mr. Schaefer** is the television director for the comedy show. Simon uses his disembodied voice as a comic tool: through the microphone, Schaefer complains about how much time Willie's and Al's artistic disagreements are costing him, and interrupts their squabble by telling them it is not in the script. ❋

# Critical Views on
## The Sunshine Boys

MARTIN GOTTFRIED ON SIMON'S UNTAPPED POTENTIAL

[Martin Gottfried, author of numerous books including *A Theater Divided: The Postwar American Stage* (1967) and *All His Jazz: The Life & Death of Bob Fosse* (1990) has contributed drama and music reviews to *Women's Wear Daily, Village Voice, The New York Post, The New York Times Magazine, Newsweek,* and others. In this excerpt, Gottfried argues that this play signals Simon's growth as a playwright because it takes a step away from upper middle class urbanity toward the richly metaphorical substance of America's vaudeville tradition.]

I have never found Neil Simon's plays as funny as his supporters have or as shallow as his detractors have. His gift for comedy is inspired, but it is as self-abused as his desire to write serious plays. His new play, "The Sunshine-Boys" (at the Broadhurst Theatre), is very different from his past work, and it promises more for the author than it does for his audience. The play is not nearly as funny as Simon can be; it tells the slimmest of stories and makes no discernible point other than being a melancholy valentine to American vaudeville. But at this stage of his career, as the most commercially successful playwright in the history of the theater, another hit cannot mean very much to him. (When one laughs his way to the bank, the laughter is invariably hollow.) "The Sunshine Boys" demonstrates Simon's first discovery of a real reason to write a play—an appreciation of old-time comics—and his first creation of a real character—one of those comics.

   This character is Willie Clark, once half of the successful comedy team of Lewis and Clark, now involuntarily retired, the victim of changing styles and failing capacities. Cranky, lecherous, lonely but still funny, he whines away in his solitary hotel room, living only for the weekly visits by a nephew who brings him some semblance of adulation for his past glories. For 12 years, he has been estranged from the one friend who would mean the most, his ex-partner, Al Lewis.

In conceiving Clark and making him the representative of a wonderful, obsolete American tradition, Simon has been more of a playwright than he was in writing any of his previous comedies.

The faceless, inhuman characters of his past plays—no more than mouthpieces for his wisecracks—and the bland urban settings of their invisible stories have now been replaced with a place (a rambling room in a seedy theatrical hotel), a specific and unusual way of life worth recalling, and a subject that is interesting to deal with. The bygone American show business tradition, as Simon wisely realized, was not only rich and artistic; but also is of considerable metaphorical quality and could well be raised to a mythic level. "The Sunshine Boys" only approaches doing full justice to the possibilities of its theme, but in choosing that theme and in going however far as he has with it, Simon has taken a great step.

The plot of "The Sunshine Boys" is slender, Clark's nephew, an agent, finally gets a job for him—an appearance on a television nostalgia special. It requires a reunion of the team, and the old man reluctantly agrees to it. When the ex-cronies get together, their quarreling picks up where it had left off. Ultimately, they do one of their routines, and this was Simon's greatest problem—to write a classic vaudeville sketch. Is it to be a pastiche? Is it to be original? Is it to be truly terrific or truly terrible? He did not solve the problem, didn't answer those questions; the Lewis and Clark routine is not original, terrific, terrible, funny or a pastiche. It is simply a doctor's office-sketch very much like a Smith and Dale routine, a disappointment surely to the author but a very difficult challenge that he wasn't quite up to. But it did take a creative playwrighting mind to think up the challenge, and that is an example of why this play should mean more to Simon than to its audience. On the other hand, the play has an ending that is sentimentally sad, unworthy of the play's ambition and unsatisfying as theater.

—Martin Gottfried, "The Sunshine Boys," *Women's Wear Daily* (22 December 1972). In *New York Theatre Critics Reviews* (1972): p. 135.

## Edwin Wilson on Comedy Rooted in Misfortune

[Edwin Wilson has interviewed many notables such as Tony Randall and Wendy Wasserstein for City University Television, and is the co-author of *Living Theater: An Introduction to Theater History* (1983). In this excerpt, Wilson suggests that Simon creates exemplary comedy by rendering it empathetic with "modern angst."]

Many things have changed about the New York theater in the last decade, but not Neil Simon; he has had a new play on Broadway every year since 1960, most of them comedies and most of them hits. One has to go back to George Abbott and the 1930s to find a record which even comes close.

His new offering, "The Sunshine Boys," which just opened at the Broadhurst Theater, assures him of a run well into 1973, if not beyond. It is Simon at the top of his form—probably his best play since "The Odd Couple," with which it has certain affinities.

"The Sunshine Boys" concerns an ex-vaudeville team, Al Lewis and Willie Clark ⟨. . .⟩

Rather than putting a damper on the play, as one might expect, Willie's misfortune provides Simon with the material on which he thrives. Simon's comedy is rooted in misfortune. His plays may be funny, sometimes wildly funny, but they are not happy. (Take the ironic title, "The Sunshine Boys," for a start.) It is out of misery and the struggle to overcome it that he fashions humor. "I laugh to keep from crying." This is why he has no protagonists, only antagonists. And the more there is to fight against, the funnier Simon can be.

In "The Prisoner of Second Avenue" it was one man against New York City. When he has two antagonists to rub together, as he did in "The Odd Couple" and does here, he can make the sparks fly.

"The Sunshine Boys" is successful because Simon is playing in his home ball park, not only with the characters and the situation, but with the milieu. It is all New York, all show business and he is on firm footing with both. There are pro-New York, anti-New Jersey lines: "I wish they had never finished the George Washington Bridge." There are running gags: Willie can never remember the names of his nephew's two children (Sandra and Marshall? Susan and Gilbert? etc.). There are visual gags: a silent, comic ballet when the two men set up furniture for a rehearsal—every time the first puts a chair in place and turns away, the second moves it across the room, meanwhile, the first moves a coat rack the second has just put in place, and so on.

Perhaps most revealing of all is the skit Simon writes for the old vaudeville team—a doctor routine ("I went to Columbia Medical School." "Did you pass?" "Yes." "You should have gone inside.") Interestingly enough, these lines are not too different from many in the play itself. What saves Simon's one-liners, great as they are, from seeming to be simply a re-run of a 30s comedy is the way he blends old jokes with modern angst. This is his secret, and he has given the formula free rein here.

Aiding the play is the production, which could hardly be better. Under Alan Arkin's direction it has pace, timing, and tremendous energy. Jack Albertson and Sam Levene as Willie and Al, and Lewis J. Stadlen as the nephew are right there with every pained expression and quick retort, right on target. They are actors as well as comics.

When Simon misses, as he has at times in the past, his characters are mean-spirited and his humor ready-made. Here he has not really changed his formula, he has just made it work. "The Sunshine Boys" is not the sunniest play around, but it is without doubt the funniest.

—Edwin Wilson, "Another Winner for Neil Simon," *The Wall Street Journal* (22 December 1972). In *New York Theatre Critics Reviews* (1972): p. 136.

SHEILA ENNIS GEITNER ON GENUINE PATHOS IN THE PLAY

[In this excerpt, Geitner argues that Simon's play can be enjoyed either on a superficial level or with full understanding of its tragic elements.]

"Spend a few afternoons around the Friars Club, a hangout for aging comedians, and a pencil, a pad, and a discriminating ear will record for you some of the funniest and saddest dialogue you ever heard," suggests Simon in his preface to Edythe McGovern's *Not-So-Simple Neil Simon* (1978). While everyone cannot spend an afternoon at the Friars Club, one has only to see *The Sunshine Boys* (1972) for a poignant, comic look at those aging comedians. It is the story of a retired and estranged vaudevillian comedy team, Willie Clark and Al Lewis, and the efforts of Ben Silverman, Clark's nephew, to reunite the pair for a special television appearance. *The Sunshine Boys* is one of Simon's favorites; in a *Playboy* interview he referred to it as his best work so far. Critics were enthusiastic about the play, giving Simon credit for his profound comic vision. William Empson, in writing about John Gay's *The Beggar's Opera* (1728), said a comedy could be "stupidly enjoyed" by those who are ignorant of its social or satirical intents. By this token *The Sunshine Boys,* with its vaudevillian dialogue and sketches, can entertain and amuse those who are unaware that Willie Clark and Al Lewis are faced with very real and painful problems. But for the more sensitive viewer, Simon offers an accurate and sympathetic account of the tolls of old age: failing health, forced retirement, absentmindedness, and relatives with good intentions who do not know what to do with old people. Willie Clark represents the struggle against encroaching age: he stubbornly refuses to move from a depressing apartment, though it is clear he is being victimized by his landlord. Al Lewis represents resignation to old age: he has meekly moved in with his daughter in New Jersey (a fate worse than death for a die-hard New Yorker). Ben Silverman must somehow reconcile these two "mighty opposites." He fails as far as the television show goes, but at the end of the play it is determined that Clark will move into the actors' retirement home. Quite by coincidence Lewis is making the same move.

The final moments of *The Sunshine Boys* contain genuine pathos. Although Lewis and Clark continue to spar with each other, it is apparent that the two share great affection and tenderness. Also, there is a tone of quiet acceptance in their voices, as if the two have embraced their old humor as a steadying influence in a time of bewildering changes.

—Sheila Ennis Geitner, "Neil Simon," *Dictionary of Literary Biography, vol 7: Twentieth-Century American Dramatists,* ed. John Mac-Nicholas (Detroit, MI: Gale Research Company, 1981): p. 258.

## DANIEL WALDEN ON SIMON'S RECREATION OF YIDDISH THEATRE

[Daniel Walden is the author and editor of numerous books, including the forthcoming *Conversations with Chaim Potok (Literary Conversations Series)*, and he has published scholarly articles on authors such as Bernard Malamud, Cynthia Ozick and Saul Bellow. He is Professor Emeritus of American Studies, English and Comparative Literature at Pennsylvania State University. In this excerpt, Walden describes the Jewish cultural milieu from which comics like Neil Simon have emerged.]

Modern American Jewish humor has its roots in the humor of the *shtetlach,* the Jewish ghettoes of Eastern Europe. Based on a recognition of the power of the surrounding community and the helplessness of the Jews, it fused sentiment with irony and self-satire with earthiness. Alienated from the mainstream, pressured to convert, lacerated by persecutions and pogroms, Jews in the nineteenth century used religion, folklore, fantasy, mysticism, and humor to survive and, almost miraculously, flourish.

From this cultural milieu, several generations of Jewish comics and writers have emerged. Jack Benny, Eddie Cantor, Georgie Jessel, Smith and Dale and so many more came out of the Lower East Side, one generation away from Eastern Europe. Woody Allen, Jerry Lewis, Soupy Sales, Lenny Bruce, Joan Rivers, David Steinberg, and Don Rickles are their heirs. Intellectually overdeveloped at the same time they are emotionally and sexually underdeveloped (or sexually overdeveloped), these stand-up comics are urban, sharp, sophisticated, infantile, arrogant. So, too, are the Jewish-style comedies of Neil Simon. ⟨. . .⟩

Smith and Dale are among the most famous vaudeville teams in the history of the American stage. Their Dr. Krankheit sketch, at the beginning of the century, still draws laughs on records and in its disguised version in *The Sunshine Boys.* There is no doubt that Al Lewis and Willie Clark are patterned after Smith and Dale, but it is also possible that Lewis and Clark (their name recalls the early nineteenth-century explorers) are meant to remind us of the great performers of the past and the way they carried on through thick and thin, often beyond the time when they should have quit. ⟨. . .⟩

Their sketch, "The Doctor and the Tax Collector," done in Yiddish inflections and using Jewish humor, depends on mispronunciations and misused words, and many references to the size of the nurse's anatomy, fore and aft. In addition, because Willie believes that some sounds are funny, a "K" occurs in almost all the names: Willie plays Dr. Klockmeyer, Al plays Kornheiser, the patient is Mrs. Kolodny, and the nurse is Miss MacKintosh. Of all Simon's plays, *The Sunshine Boys* is probably the earthiest, the one closest to Yiddish theater. In the heyday of vaudeville, the Jewish comedy teams were often crude, even bawdy, but they were always in tune with the audience, and involved them in the problems of the performers.

Neil Simon, with his eyes on the reality of the past, has given us the talent of the older generation, especially reminiscent of the flavor of the Second Avenue theaters. Historically, Jews maintained unitary households, but in the New World, with success and affluence, it became easier for some young people to farm out their parents, aunts, and uncles to old-age homes. In this case, the Actors Home in New Jersey, was the alternative for Willie and Al. Joe Smith, the model for Willie, has lived there for many years. Of course, in the plot, the nephew Ben said that he was willing to take Willie in, but Willie knew that that meant moving in with Ben's family, and Willie detested kids. Willie also resented being an unwelcome guest, or at least an unlooked-for guest, in Ben's home. In any case, Simon mixes humor and tragedy. The two old performers hated each other but secretly admired and loved each other. They also needed attention, they needed people to fuss over them, they needed to be made to feel that they were still human beings. This title suggests warmth and energy, given freely by all in the way the sun has sustained us all. But behind the title is Simon's feeling for the situational conflict, the irony in the plight of the talented elderly who are to be honored and admired for what they gave to their era. In Eastern Europe the extended family was common, old people were organic parts of the household because the family was essential to Judaism. America broke down the old ways. The conflict was plain to see. Indeed this was a humorous situation in which pain was involved. *The Sunshine Boys,* embedded in the Jewish experience, is a sad tale told humorously.

—Daniel Walden, "Neil Simon's Jewish-Style Comedies," *From Hester Street to Hollywood: The Jewish-American Stage and Screen,* ed. Sarah Blacher Cohen (Bloomington: University of Indiana Press, 1983): pp. 152, 158–160.

# C. W. E. Bigsby on Sparring Characters

[C. W. E. Bigsby, author of the three-volume study *A Critical Introduction to Twentieth-Century American Drama* (1982) and *David Mamet* (1985), is Professor of American Studies at the University of East Anglia. In this excerpt, Bigsby points to Simon's expertise in staging oppositional characters with detachment by comparing this play to *The Odd Couple*.]

Starting with *Come Blow Your Horn* in 1961 he created a seemingly unbroken line of successful comedies. As a former gag-writer he tended to pepper his plays with effective one-liners, but the social observation was sharp and the situations simultaneously reassuring and disturbingly familiar. Almost invariable the angry blow is deflected, the wounding remark parried, the trauma avoided but the vulnerabilities are identified with such accuracy that from time to time there is the suggestion of another playwright locked inside the Jewish comedian. It is that fact which, perhaps paradoxically, has sharpened the edge of his humour, as in *The Old Couple* and *The Sunshine Boys.*

Trying to explain the basis of his art he recalled an argument with his wife in which their very relationship made them adepts at the wounding remark. At the height of their exchange his wife had thrown a frozen lamb chop at him, striking him a glancing blow. The absurdity of the situation defused the pain. It seems a particularly telling observation, for that is the quality of his work which is most compelling. He is as accurate as his wife in hurling lamb chops and as adept at recognizing vulnerabilities and absurdities as he had proved on that occasion. By the same token his technique of deflecting pain through humour accounts for both his popular appeal and the critical suspicion that he inspires. Where Beckett's and Pinter's humour leads to the centre of the pain Simon's leads away from it. When he speaks of 'two people on a stage, both of whom cared for each other, but were unable or unwilling to yield or to submit without having first gained some small vicious victory' he identifies a human truth which too often becomes his comic means rather than his dramatic end. The blood in a Neil Simon play is seldom real blood and it is a rare pain which does not come with an analgesic of wit. Just as Simon described himself in his argument with his wife, as outside looking in, 'no longer involved as a man in conflict, but as an observer, an audience, so to speak, watching two people on a stage', so there is a sense in which his characters become vaudevillians—in *The Sunshine Boys,* literally so—self-consciously performing their lives as an alternative to living them.

In looking for an analogy for his own ability to step back from a situation in order to take a detached view of human absurdities, Simon referred to Lord Cardigan and Lord Raglan in the Crimean War. The choice was an interesting one, for the fact is that there is a battle of sorts in most of his plays, a fencing, a manoeuvring for advantage which is the root of the comedy and equally of the pain which the comedy denies. Though many of his plays have large casts there is a tendency for him to focus on the sparring between two individuals who use language as weapons, and who need one another to give meaning to their repartee. That need, which goes beyond language, is a hint of something in Simon's plays which continues to fascinate.

> —C. W. E. Bigsby, *Modern American Drama, 1945–1990* (Cambridge and New York: Cambridge University Press, 1992): pp. 157–8.

ELLEN SCHIFF ON ENCODING JEWISH CONTENT

[Ellen Schiff is Professor Emerita of French and world literature at Massachusetts College of Liberal Arts at North Adams. She has published numerous articles on Jews in the theatre and edited *Awake and Singing: Seven Classic Plays from the American Jewish Repertoire* (1995) and *Fruitful and Multiplying; Nine Contemporary Plays from the American Jewish Repertoire* (1996). In this excerpt, Schiff contextualizes Simon's work within American Jewish playwriting by demonstrating how this play borrows their methods of manifesting Jewish content.]

Like Simon, these dramatists also wrote in genres other than the legitimate theatre. Like Simon, they did not always write plays with Jewish content. However, when they did incorporate Jewish material in their works, they and their colleagues did so in a number of readily identifiable ways. The Simon canon contains examples of virtually all of them.

One of the hallmarks of American Jewish playwriting is its variability in being explicit about Jewish characters and situations. Concern for the widest acceptability has motivated authors to adopt two opposite ways of encoding. Both leave it to astute theatergoers who pick up the clues and determine how Jewishness shapes characters' situation or behavior.

The first is the practice of populating scripts with characters who have Jewish names, but minimal Jewish substance. Kaufman and Ferber's Sigmund Rosenblatt in *Merton of the Movies* (1922), Isaac and Sadie Cohen in John Howard Lawson's *Processional* (1925), along with Ben and Belle Stark in Clifford Odets's *Rocket To the Moon* (1938), figure among the antecedents of more recent characters like Shelly Levene (David Mamet's *Glengarry Glen Ross,* 1982), Moe Baum and Fanny Margolies (Arthur Miller's *The American Clock,* 1982)—as well as Sam Nash and Jesse Kiplinger in Simon's *Plaza Suite,* Herb and Libby Tucker in *I Ought to Be in Pictures, Rumors'* Lenny Ganz, and Barney Cashman, the titular *Last of the Red Hot Lovers.*

On the flip side of this practice, characters are given Jewish speech patterns, lifestyles, personality traits, or values—but neutral, sometimes deliberately non-Jewish names. Samuel Shipman calls his shrewd glove salesmen in *Cheaper To Marry* (1924) Jim Knight and Charlie Tyler. An overbearing matriarch in Rose Franken's *Another Language* (1931) dominates the lives of her married children; Jewish speech patterns and telltale attitudes and practices notwithstanding, this clan is known as the Hallams. The violinist who must choose between art and material success in Odets's *Golden Boy* (1937) is called Joe Bonaparte. Doubtless the most familiar example is the Loman family in *Death of a Salesman,* whose ethnicity still provokes vigorous debate. Characters with homogenized names in subsequent Arthur Miller plays, like *After the Fall* (1964) and *Clara* (1986), also display speech patterns and concerns that sound distinctly Jewish. ⟨. . .⟩

Simon plays mischievously with names in *The Sunshine Boys* in which the word "Jewish" also does not appear. The title characters, Willie Clark and Al Lewis, are recognizably modeled on the famous Jewish entertainers Joe Smith (né Sulzer) and Charlie Dale (né Marks). In this valentine to vaudeville (and to his own background, writing for stand-up comedians), Simon trumps all his predecessors, actual and fictional, who have disguised their Jewish names. First he dubs uncle and nephew Willie and Ben, inevitably recalling the ill-matched brothers in Miller's quintessential American (Jewish?) play. But Simon does Miller—as well as Smith and Dale—one better with his comedians' last names. Who could be more American than Lewis and Clark?

—Ellen Schiff, "Funny, He *Does* Look Jewish," *Neil Simon: A Casebook,* ed. Gary Konas (New York: Garland Publishing, Inc., 1997): pp. 48–50.

# Plot Summary of
## *Lost in Yonkers*

*Lost in Yonkers,* set in 1942 as World War II draws near, stages the suffering of a family controlled by a hardened Grandma Kurnitz. A German Jewish emigrant who suffered torturous conditions in the old country, Grandma has steeled herself against the world. Ironically selling sweets to the community, the emotionless Grandma has raised her children to survive, but not to live. Having grown up without even a hint of affection or play, her children Louie, Eddie, Bella and Gert have adapted—but not without serious emotional handicaps. In a starkly comedic way, Neil Simon portrays the vicious cycle of misplaced rage that wracks many a dysfunctional family, while locating the source of that pain, as critics have noted, in German anti-semitism.

The play takes place in an apartment above "Kurnitz's Kandy Store" in Yonkers, New York. As **Act One, Scene One** begins, fifteen year-old Jay and thirteen year-old Arty wait in the living room as their father discusses their future with their grandmother in the bedroom. As they wait, they rehearse some of the family folklore. Their grandmother is deaf in one ear and is known to swing her cane like an expert golf player. Aunt Bella, one of her adult daughters, is semi-retarded from being hit in the head by her mother's cane so many times. Aunt Gertrude, suffering from a lifelong terror of Grandma, sucks air compulsively when she talks. Uncle Louie is a henchman for the mob who collects and delivers large bags of money.

Bella, who still lives with Grandma, enters enthusiastically to greet Jay and Arty. Described as "warm and congenial as she is emotionally arrested," she dotes on the boys. But she is temperamental and insistent, which seems rooted in a combination of her stunted emotional growth and her inability to register the boys' having advanced in age since she last saw them. Eddie comes out of the bedroom to inform the boys of his plan. He has gone into debt with a loan shark because of the high costs of caring for their late mother, who died of cancer. He must leave them in the care of his mother while he travels to the South in search of work. Thanks to the war overseas, he can sell scrap iron to the factories and make enough money in a year to pay back the loan shark. He asks the boys to help him by complying with their grandmother, and despite their fear, they agree.

Grandmother, at least 70 years old, is instantly terrifying: "Authority and discipline seem to be her overriding characteristics and she would command attention in a crowd." She interrogates the two boys with her "clear German accent" and decides to take them, but not without citing Eddie's pusillanimous character and shameful lack of loyalty to the family. Insulted, Eddie refuses to let them stay; but Bella insists, threatening to leave Grandma if they cannot stay.

In **Scene Two**, Jay and Arty learn in a letter that their father has developed an irregular heartbeat and begin to devise schemes for helping him raise the money he needs. The following Sunday afternoon (**Scene Three**) Bella tells the boys her secret: a theater usher who is mentally handicapped like her has proposed marriage to her. They plan to open a restaurant together, and Bella hopes to finance the project by asking Grandma for $5,000. She reveals that Grandma keeps at least $10,000 hidden in the house somewhere. One week later (**Scene Four**), Jay searches the candy store in the middle of the night for the money, without success. Uncle Louie, who has been hiding out in the candy store, enters in full mobster dress. Through the character of Louie, Simon provides comic relief; this is a man whose bullying exterior only thinly veils his laughable cowardice and immaturity. Claiming to be hiding out from some mobsters who disapprove of his choice of girlfriend, his tales of mob life (including a spirited "moxie" pose) seem best fitted for the playground at recess. A prime vehicle of Simon's talent for comic irony, Jay acts the adult and humors his uncle as he gives each boy $5 to deny knowing his whereabouts when the other henchmen come looking for him.

**Act Two** opens with Eddie's voice over, explaining in a letter to his sons that he is in the hospital for exhaustion. Arty is home sick from school, and Grandma forces him to drink her curative but detestable soup. Arty puts up a considerable fight, telling her to take her anger out on Hitler. Impressed by Arty's "moxie," Louie enters after Grandma leaves and tells him a story of being locked in a closet as a child for hours, thereby being cured of the need to cry ever again. In a moment that highlights the theme of ineffective parenting and its disastrous results, Louie explains to Arty that Grandma desperately wanted to save her children from pain by training them not to feel. He reveals that a horse fell on Grandma's foot during a political rally in Berlin when she was twelve years old. She never fixed it, and she has not taken an aspirin yet. Louie's story shows how Grandma has displaced all her emotional pain onto her foot—the foot she did not fix so she could save money to escape to America after losing her husband and two children. By squeezing all that pain into her foot rather than her heart, she diminishes its power to destroy her.

Knowing that Louie will leave that night, Jay asks him to hire him and take him on as an assistant so that he can make enough money to save his father. Louie refuses; a boy with so much "moxie" should not be taken away from a family to whom he is such a great asset.

In **Scene Two**, Bella has gathered the whole family for a "talk." She reveals to the family her plans to marry her new boyfriend and help him open a restaurant. She wants to have children of her own and plans to teach them to be happy. She begs Grandma to help her, but Grandma leaves the room wordlessly.

The following week (**Scene Three**) Aunt Bella has left the house and has been hiding out at Aunt Gert's house, crying for two days. Grandma is tired and upset, and Jay and Arty try to cheer her up. Aunt Bella returns, ready to talk now that she has no tears left. Bella reveals that when she was growing up she let boys and men touch her because she never got any affection at home. Though she admits to being somewhat of a child, she needs Grandma to understand that she also has a woman's needs. She returns the $5000 she stole from Grandma. When Bella tells Grandma that she has ruined her children, and that the two children who died were the lucky ones, she cracks Grandma's shell. Grandma admits that after losing Rose and Aaron, her two deceased children, she stopped feeling because she could not stand losing any more. She is willing to admit that she may not have done right by Bella. Bella's boyfriend, meanwhile, has decided that he does not want to get married. Bella will continue to stay with Grandma, but things will never be the same because of her foray into the adult world.

Nine months later (**Scene Four**) Eddie has returned from successfully raising the money to pay the loan shark back. Louie is fighting in the South Pacific. Grandma tells Eddie she is proud of him for fulfilling his obligations and not looking for handouts. Eddie promises that he and the kids will no longer be the strangers to Grandma that they were before he left. Grandma, who never misses anything, tells the boys she saw them searching for her money that dark night. In what could be construed as a half jest, she tells them they should have looked behind the malted machine. When Eddie and the boys have left, we get a glimpse of Bella's new self-confidence. She is now in the practice of inviting friends over for dinner and playing music. As the curtain closes, Grandma is alone on stage nodding as if to say "so it's come to this . . ." Though Grandma will never be an affectionate type, her stony exterior has been softened a bit by the very children she has taught to be cold and hard. Likewise, Neil Simon's comic perspective has alleviated for the audience the pain of watching a play that shows how one injustice (the Holocaust) begets another (Grandma's household). ❀

# List of Characters in
## *Lost in Yonkers*

**Grandma Kurnitz** is an elderly German Jewish immigrant. As a result of enduring anti-semitism and losing her husband and two of her children, she has not allowed herself to feel or succumb to pain for most of her adult life. She believes that her life represents a punishment for outliving her children. Like her feelings, all her money is hidden away in the candy store. In an effort to protect her living children, she has trained them not to feel by hardening them with punishments such as locking them in a closet or beating them with her cane. Living with Jay and Arty, being challenged by Bella's sudden rebellion against her dictates, and facing the possible demise of her son Eddie, Grandma begins to soften her rigid exterior and loosen the dictatorial control she has always exerted over them.

**Eddie Kurnitz** is Grandma's oldest son and the father of Jay and Arty. Growing up, he was abused by Grandma for being a crybaby. Her plan to harden him never worked. When he got married, his wife nurtured and supported him in a way his mother never did, so he began to stay away from Grandma. Eddie's wife has died of cancer, and in the process of taking care of her medical needs he has gone into debt with a loan shark. Desperate, he leaves his two sons with Grandma so he can make enough money to pay off the debt; in the process he develops an irregular heartbeat. When he returns to collect his children, he is ready to forgive Grandma and let her back into his family's life on a regular basis.

**Jay Kurnitz** is Eddie's fifteen year-old son. He understands the ways in which adults create protective exteriors to compensate for their fears, and is able to pierce through those exteriors with his keen insight. He sees his father's desperation, Louie's cowardice, Bella's innate goodness, and Grandma's fear. He wishes to travel with Louie so he can save his father from having to work so hard, but Louie refuses. He also tries to find Grandma's money so he can help his father. When his father returns from his trip, Jay has learned much about Grandma, and shows new respect and compassion for her.

**Arty Kurnitz** is Eddie's thirteen year-old son. He is still young enough to be carried away by Louie's "James Cagney" act and terrified of

Grandma. He is also still young enough to tell the blunt truth when asked a question, which Grandma respects. As the play progresses, he develops confidence. He tells Grandma she should take out her anger on Hitler, not on her family; and he begins to gain an understanding of the good qualities of his grandmother.

**Bella**, in her mid-thirties, is one of Grandma's daughters. Her emotional growth has been stunted, and her maturity level has been frozen at the adolescent stage. Jay and Arty believe her mental handicap is a result of being hit over the head with Grandma's cane too many times. She still lives with Grandma, much like a dependent child, yet she knows Grandma would suffer from great loneliness without her. When Bella meets a man and considers getting married, she releases years of anger at never being nurtured, touched or held. She tells Grandma that she let boys and men touch her when she was a child in an effort to get the affection she could not get at home. Though Bella does not get married, her relationship with Grandma changes because she has finally told the truth and forced Grandma to confront her greatest fears.

**Louie**, about thirty-six years old, is Grandma's son. He prides himself on always having stood up to Grandma when he was young. He believes he learned his most valuable lessons from her: how to maintain a hard exterior, never cry, and never back down to anyone. He is a henchman for the mob and is proud of his tough image. However, he comes to Grandma's house to hide out from his mob enemies, and as Jay points out, is a coward for doing so. Louie can only be tough around his family; when it comes to the outside world, he is a fraud.

**Gert**, in her mid to late thirties, is Grandma's daughter. She has an uncontrollable habit of sucking in air when she talks. Once, when trying to blow out a candle, she sucked the air back in and the candle lit up again. Her intense need to eat her words, her incredible fear of what will happen if she extends herself out to the world, comes from growing up with Grandma, who kept her in constant fear and yet would not allow her to cry. ❀

# Critical Views on
## *Lost in Yonkers*

FRANK RICH ON SIMON'S TREATMENT OF
HUMAN BRUTALITY

[Frank Rich is an op-ed columnist for *The New York Times*
and has also served as the paper's chief drama critic. He
has written about culture and politics for many publica-
tions, including *Time, Esquire,* and *The New Republic.* In
this excerpt, Rich criticizes Simon for downplaying the
pathos of human brutality by couching it in mediocre
domestic comedy.]

Of all the odd couples created by Neil Simon in his 30-year career in
the theater, none has been less funny or more passionately acted
than the battling mother and daughter indelibly embodied by Irene
Worth and Mercedes Ruehl in "Lost in Yonkers," the writer's new
memory piece at the Richard Rodgers Theater.

Ms. Worth, her usual elegance obliterated by a silver bun of steel-
wool hair, rimless spectacles and a limping stride, is an elderly
widow known only as Grandma Kurnitz. A childhood immigrant
from Germany to the United States, she has devoted her adulthood
to the Yonkers candy store over which she makes her home. Bella,
played by Ms. Ruehl, is the 35-year-old child who never moved out
and has paid with her life. A gawky woman with an eager smile and a
confused, bubbly manner, Bella is, as one line has it, "closed for
repairs." Her mind isn't quite right, her existence is bounded by the
soda counter, and her development is arrested in early adolescence.

There's some humor in this, but, as one character remarks of Ms.
Worth's Grandma, "I never said she was a lot of laughs." One doesn't
have to be of German Jewish descent to recognize this ice-cold
woman who yanks her face away from anyone who tries to plant a
kiss on it and who belittles any relative who attempts to puncture
her scowling reserve. She is terrifying, and not primarily because she
wields a mean cane. As acted with matchless precision by Ms. Worth,
Grandma is a nearly silent killer whose steely monstrousness can be
found in the emotions she withholds rather than in whatever faint
feelings she might grudgingly express.

As nature dictates, Bella is her opposite, and Ms. Ruehl imbues her with a vulnerability as electric in its way as the comic ferocity she so memorably brought to the role of a hellbent Mafia wife in Jonathan Demme's film "Married to the Mob." All elbows and knees, Ms. Ruehl seems to jitterbug constantly about the parlor, thirsting for any experience or human contact, however small and humdrum, that might come her way before her mother snuffs it out.

Grandma and Bella are on a collision course, and when the blowout arrives, it not only brings "Lost in Yonkers" to a wrenching catharsis, but it also wipes out much of the nostalgically sentimental family portrait that Mr. Simon presented to Broadway audiences in his autobiographical trilogy of the 1980s. Whatever the virtues of the author's Brighton Beach plays, they always seemed a little too roseate to be true. The relatives on stage were guilty of pecadilloes and frailties, never major crimes. That's not the case here, where the only lines referring to the family as a safe haven are bitterly ironic. Grandma has a crushed foot—from her Berlin childhood—and she is out to get revenge on the world by crushing anyone or anything in her path. While Mr. Simon's autobiographical cycle officially ended with "Broadway Bound," it is in "Lost in Yonkers" that he seems at last to be baring the most fundamental scar of all, that of a child rejected by a parent.

I don't see how anyone can fail to be moved by the sight of Ms. Ruehl, the lonely repository of this grief, when she stands center stage in Act II of "Lost in Yonkers," crying and begging for the intimacy, physical and otherwise, she has always been so cruelly denied. If this play kept its focus on Bella and Grandma throughout, one might even be able to mention it in the same paragraph, if not necessarily the same breath, as "The Glass Menagerie," "The Effect of Gamma Rays on Man-in-the-Moon Marigolds" and "Gypsy," among other American classics about lethal mothers and oppressed daughters. But Mr. Simon, whether by sloppiness or design, falls considerably short of this hallowed territory. If he is no longer camouflaging human brutality, he is still packaging it within a lot of fluff, and not always his best fluff at that. While the gripping Grandma-Bella drama is never quite lost in "Lost in Yonkers," it is too frequently crowded out by domestic comedy of a most ordinary sort.

—Frank Rich, "Simon on Love Denied," *The New York Times* (22 February 1991). In *New York Theatre Critics Reviews* (1991): p. 376.

# CLIVE BARNES ON THE HAPPY ENDING

[Clive Barnes, author of many books including *Inside American Ballet Theatre* (1983) and editor of *Best American Plays* (Seventh and Eighth Series 1975, 1983) has contributed music, drama, dance and film reviews to *Daily Express* (London), *The Spectator* (London), *The New York Times* and *The New York Post*. In this excerpt, Barnes argues that the play's happy ending lightens its tragic load in the manner of a Hollywood movie or television show.]

The motto of the family is survival—the grandmother survived anti-Semitism in Germany, Louie will survive the mob, Eddie will survive the South, and everyone will survive Yonkers. But there's a price. As Grandma Kurnitz firmly believes: "You don't survive in this world unless you're like steel." And love and steel make poor partners.

What happens is less important than who it happens to—often the sign of a good play and superior writing—and although Simon sometimes risks an over-glib gag (though even these stay in character) he doesn't really put a foot wrong until the very last scene.

The set-up is Chekhovian. The pay-off is TV/Hollywood at its schmaltziest. Nothing, kids, is as bad as it seems. Even Uncle Louie has the chance to end up a hero. Tragedy has gone with the wind, and even the wind is only mild flatulence. A pity. "Lost in Yonkers" could have been a contender in a league Simon hasn't previously played in, except for that tryout with "The Ginger-bread Lady."

Nevertheless, a happy ending never hurt anyone, especially those going to a box-office or walking to a bank. On its own terms "Lost in Yonkers" is perfectly splendid, and I am a mean grouch to let my initial enchantment dribble off into slight, if crucial, disappointment.

Like the play itself, Gene Saks' flawlessly idiomatic and seamless staging, and Loquasto's designs, the impeccable (really impeccable) acting should, when the time comes, reap a sheaf of Tony nominations. Indeed, it's difficult to say who wouldn't deserve one.

In the two leading roles, Irene Worth as the grandmother—both Teutonic and Jewish, with an accent that could break stones and a manner to freeze the Rhine—and Mercedes Ruehl wonderfully fragile and vulnerable as Bella, offer performances fit for the history books. They are remarkable. Until the undernourishment of their last scene, they live in flesh and blood.

Kevin Spacey as Uncle Louie is almost as sensational, sparring his way through the play like a cocky little boxer who knows the fight is fixed but is not sure which way, while Mark Blum as the wimpish father, and Lauren Klein as the aunt with a psychosomatic voice, are both admirable.

And how is it that Simon can write so well for adolescents? And how well the two adolescents here in question, Jamie Marsh as the elder brother and Danny Gerard as the kid, take all the golden opportunities offered!

So Neil Simon has done it again, with a craftsmanship and skill probably unmatched in the contemporary English-speaking theater. Why should we want him to do more? Because his work so often suggests that he can.

—Clive Barnes, "Lost in Yonkers, Happily Ever After," *New York Post* (22 February 1991). In *New York Theatre Critics Reviews* (1991): pp. 377–378.

## HOWARD KISSEL ON SURVIVAL AND SELF-SACRIFICE

[Howard Kissel, author of *David Merrick: The Abominable Showman: The Unauthorized Biography* (1993), has served as the chief theater critic for the *New York Daily News* and was for fifteen years the Arts Editor of *Women's Wear Daily*. In this excerpt, Kissell suggests that survival and self-sacrifice are Grandma's essential motivations, and that Simon stages these stereotypically Jewish traits impressively.]

⟨. . .⟩ The play focuses on an elderly German-Jewish woman, the matriarch of a family that includes a retarded, pathetically affectionate daughter; a gangster son; a daughter whose breathing goes haywire whenever she visits the dowager, and a son whose spirit the mother has broken, but who, in the course of the play, finds a new strength.

At first, the woman seems more German than Jewish. She came of age in Berlin before World War I and her iron will, her punctiliousness make her seem more a disciple of Bismarck and Clausewitz than a daughter of Zion.

And yet, when she finally—almost contemptuously—speaks in her own defense, we see that what has motivated her has been an obsession with survival.

Moreover, though she does not luxuriate in self-sacrifice in the way that has inspired countless Jewish Mother jokes, we eventually see, to our surprise, that she is profoundly capable of it.

Survival and self-sacrifice have traditionally been Jewish concerns. By addressing them without the usual Jewish stereotypes or cozy humor, Simon has written an unusually tough play.

It is also a wonderfully theatrical one. Gene Saks has directed the play with an intensity and imagination that mine its riches splendidly.

As the mother, Irene Worth assumes the dimensions of a prehistoric monster, her features already rigidified in an ice age of her own creation. She lugs herself around as if she were dragging chains: She is indeed encumbered by a sacrifice she made years ago, a sacrifice she has confided in no one.

Her head is invariably cocked in an air of imperious condescension, like the ruler of some duchy, which, in fact, she is. Worth makes this petty, difficult but ultimately well-intentioned woman seem, as she should, someone of stature.

Mercedes Ruehl, who made such a sexy impression in "Other People's Money," is extraordinarily moving as the gangly, slightly goofy, poignantly generous daughter, particularly in a speech in the second act where she makes clear her own understanding of her plight.

Kevin Spacey plays the gangster with a mesmerizing finesse that only accentuates the menace he represents.

Jamie Marsh, as the older of the two boys, has a face with a remarkable capacity to register varying degrees of horror, all of which have comic impact. As the younger boy, Danny Gerard gives a wonderfully bravura performance. The wrinkled brow of Mark Blum, who plays their father, is as accurate an index of potential ulcers as any hospital chart. Lauren Klein brings great warmth to the role of the aunt with the erratic larynx.

Santo Loquasto sets the tone of the play with his Hopper-like scrim suggesting nostalgia and dislocation. He conveys Simon's darkly comic mood in the plainly furnished apartment and the extroverted costumes.

"Lost in Yonkers" is one of Simon's most impressive and funniest plays.

—Howard Kissel, "'Lost' Finds Simon in Top Form," *Daily News* (22 February 1991). In *New York Theatre Critics Reviews* (1991): pp. 378–9.

## JACK KROLL ON THE AUTOBIOGRAPHICAL ASPECTS OF THE PLAY

[Jack Kroll is a noted drama and movie critic who has written for *Newsweek* and *New York Magazine*. In this excerpt, Kroll explains the role Simon's own pain has played in the creation of this darker play.]

In *Lost in Yonkers* Neil Simon has found himself. For all their popularity, his recent "autobiographical" trilogy—"Brighton Beach Memoirs," "Biloxi Blues," "Broadway Bound"—didn't succeed in stitching Simon the Funny and Simon the Serious into a new creature, Simon the Pure. Too often he was dishing out one from column A and one from column B: have a laugh, have a tear. In his 27th play laughter and tears have come together in a new emotional truth. There are moments in this play when you experience a new kind of laughter for Simon, a silent laughter that doesn't explode into a yuk but implodes straight into your heart.

It's 1942, and Simon gives us a nuclear family that clearly has some protons missing. Grandma Kurnitz (Irene Worth) is a fearsome German-Jewish tyrant who's terrorized her children, now grown: Bella (Mercedes Ruehl) is a good-hearted soul who's not right in the head. Gert (Lauren Klein) is so nervous that she sometimes forgets to stop talking when she inhales, so that her speech is punctuated by death rattles of fear. Eddie (Mark Blum) is panic stricken when he has to persuade Grandma to take his young sons Jay (Jamie Marsh) and Arty (Danny Gerard) so that he can go off to a defense job. Only his brother Louie (Kevin Spacey), a small-time gangster, seems unafraid of Grandma. Or is he?

Starting out bonkers in Yonkers, the family gradually deepens and darkens. These are all wounded human beings. Grandma, seemingly a monster of negativity—unloving, unfeeling, uncaring—turns out to be the most deeply wounded of all. Simon even dares to associate her with the Holocaust, and succeeds. The showdown scenes between Bella and her mother are the strongest he's ever written.

Simon finds the right tones and rhythms for three generations, and they're nailed down by his longtime director Gene Saks and an extraordinary ensemble. Worth and Ruehl dig deep and fly high. With her cane thumping as her voice fires rebuffs and reprimands, Worth embodies the casualties who've had the love battered out of them. Ruehl is piercingly funny and achingly tragic as Bella, who has a child's mind in a woman's body. This is American acting at its best.

Was there a Bella in Neil Simon's life? Only inside Simon himself. Cheerfully he admits: "When Bella tells how the kids in school would yell at her, 'Hey Bella, the Lost and Found called. Come and get your brain,' well, I've gone through periods like that, when I was totally disoriented. During the writing I went through the same pain that Bella does." One period of disorientation was the death of his first wife, Joan, from cancer at 39. "What that leaves you with is enormous guilt," he says. This led to extensive psychoanalysis. "It never cured me of anything," says Simon. "But it made me aware. Since I don't have a formal education, that was my education."

But Simon's informal education was even more important for his insight into a character like Grandma, who exerts such ruthless emotional control over her children. "My mother used to tie me into my high chair so I wouldn't fall out," he says. Many years later that feeling of constriction and control has led to a play in which a mother controls her daughter so that she won't "fall out" into a world where she can be hurt by her emotional vulnerability.

—Jack Kroll, "Going Bonkers in Yonkers," *Newsweek* (4 March 1991). In *New York Theatre Critics Reviews* (1991): p. 381.

## ELLEN SCHIFF ON GRANDMA'S PAST

[Ellen Schiff is Professor Emerita of French and world literature at Massachusetts College of Liberal Arts at North
Adams. She is the author of numerous articles on Jews in
the theatre, and she has edited *Awake and Singing: Seven
Classic Plays from the American Jewish Repertoire* (1995) and
*Fruitful and Multiplying; Nine Contemporary Plays from the
American Jewish Repertoire* (1996). In this excerpt, Schiff
places Grandma's character in the context of dramatic characters who carry the lessons of the Holocaust.]

When Grandma Kurnitz was a twelve-year-old growing up in Berlin,
a horse stepped on her foot at a Nazi rally. More than the foot was
crushed. Living with pain, fear, and death, Grandma has learned that
"You don't survive in dis vorld vitout being like steel." Like the
Jewish mothers in Depression-era plays, Odets's Bessie Berger
(*Awake and Sing!*) or Sylvia Regan's Becky Felderman (*Morning
Star*), Kurnitz understands the necessity of teaching her children
survival skills in a cruel world. Unlike her predecessors, this mater-
familias seems totally unconcerned with their emotional lives, least
of all with demonstrations of love. Her obduracy has deformed all of
her children, but it is her slightly retarded, emotionally needy
daughter Bella who bears the heaviest burden.

It is especially in the scenes between Kurnitz and Bella that Simon
"gets in the middle." Abandoning his more characteristic levity, he
plumbs the depths of Bella's desperate craving for warmth and affection. And then he makes us understand why her mother withholds
any encouragement. Perhaps she was once as warm-hearted as Bella,
but the loss of two children taught her that callousness is an effective
defense against pain.

Grandma Kurnitz had yet another lesson in learning to be "like
steel." Though the script supplies few details of her past in Germany,
it is clearly never far from her mind. At one point, she casually tells
her grandson that had he been a boy in Germany instead of Yonkers,
he would be dead by now. Grandma Kurnitz takes her place in the
company of characters in recent American Jewish plays about
parent-child relationships in families coping with the indelible
shadow of the Holocaust. It hardly seems sheer coincidence that *Lost
in Yonkers* shared the 1991 New York season with Richard Green-

berg's *The American Plan* and Jon Robin Baitz's *The Substance of Fire*. All three plays are concerned with the ways in which American-born Jews are shaped by the survival-first intransigence history forced their Nazi-scarred parents to adopt. All three take their place in a growing body of plays which draw on the consequences of the Holocaust for American Jewry, spared the horror but not its lessons.

The distance between Alan Baker's apartment in the East Sixties to Kurnitz's Kandy Store in Yonkers is far greater than any map would indicate. Simon has travelled a long road between the two addresses. En route, he has often pulled up alongside other American Jewish playwrights. Works like the trilogy and *Yonkers* indicate that now, like Baitz, Greenberg, Tony Kushner, Donald Margulies, and Elizabeth Swados, among others, who write frankly out of their lives as Jews, he's keeping an eye on his rear-view mirror. He's looking to see how where he's come from leads into where he's going. Or as he told the *New York Times* when *Lost in Yonkers* won the Pulitzer, "The play came out of instinctive feelings I had and probably wakened in me things I didn't know about" (Interview). It turns out that being funny isn't the only result of being born in the Bronx, in the Depression, and Jewish.

—Ellen Schiff, "Funny, He *Does* Look Jewish," *Neil Simon: A Casebook*, ed. Gary Konas (New York: Garland Publishing, Inc., 1997): pp. 56–57.

## BETTE MANDL ON THE PLAY'S HOLOCAUST THEME

[Bette Mandl, Professor of English at Suffolk University, Boston, has published numerous scholarly articles on Eugene O'Neill and other authors. In this excerpt, Mandl argues that Grandma's house in Yonkers becomes a psychological testing ground for two young boys learning the ways of a world shaped by the Holocaust.]

*Lost in Yonkers* is set in 1942, and not only are its characters identifiably Jewish, but the darker aspects of the Jewish experience of the time find their way into it. The play is shaped around several months in the lives of two engaging young brothers, Jay and Arty, whose mother has died and whose father is compelled to leave them with their formidable grandmother, and their affectionate but limited Aunt Bella, in order to go across the country selling scrap metal. Though he maintains a balance in *Lost in Yonkers* between the humorous and the poignant, Simon approaches themes that were often conspicuously absent from theatre for many years of its postwar history. The horrors of the war in 1942, which were then yet to be fully known, remain outside of the play's domain, but the Holocaust casts its shadow on this work.

Even minimal acknowledgments of the Holocaust in film and theatre are highly charged, and become implicated in the larger concerns that surround the collective memory of the Shoah. Nonetheless, with increasing frequency the Holocaust is invoked, even in works shaped for popular entertainment, and often in apparently casual ways. In Wendy Wasserstein's 1992 play *The Sisters Rosensweig*, for example, a brief reference to the Holocaust surfaces in the midst of banter about issues of identity and relationships. Merv, who is courting Sara, the most determinedly assimilated of the three American Jewish sisters of the play, says, "Sometimes I look at you and see all my mother's photographs of her mother and her mother's entire family. . . . Unfortunately most of them and their families didn't survive." Such lines provide audiences with a psychological jolt, as well as a demand for a swift return to present pleasures from the brief reminder of unthinkable atrocities. Wasserstein's play could not bear the weight of fuller revelation about the Holocaust, but the allusion suggests that it is intrinsic to her characters' experience of the world.

There are a number of such moments in *Lost in Yonkers*. One example occurs in an exchange between Jay and Arty, who wonder how they might manage to secure some money for their father, then traveling in the South to earn a living for them. Jay remembers talk of an uncle in Poland who had left Eddie an inheritance, but Arty, the younger brother, already senses enough about their situation to say, "You think the Germans would let some Jew in Poland send nine thousand dollars to some Jew in Alabama?" Here what is barely more than a humorous aside leaves the audience to recall for themselves what will not be fully introduced, even as they laugh on cue.

*Lost in Yonkers* is linked with those works in which a quip pointing in the direction of what appalls suffices as a reminder of the Shoah. I would suggest, however, that the play's design allows it to go further. The Holocaust emerges as a theme in *Lost in Yonkers* through an intriguing displacement, which disguises what would otherwise be too disturbing. The domestic world the boys enter in Yonkers becomes a kind of psychological theatre for them, where, as they face the problems of their family predicament, they simultaneously master an anxiety about a larger world filled with untold risks for those just like themselves. Through a complex portrait of the grandmother, Simon manages to bring the war, and its particular terrors for Jews, closer to home.

⟨. . .⟩ In the stage directions, Grandma Kurnitz's description sets her apart from other women, and, in particular, Jewish women in maternal roles: "Authority and discipline seem to be her overriding characteristics and she would command attention in a crowd. She speaks with few but carefully chosen words, with a clear German accent." Her rather masculine bearing and her accent mark her as a familial symbol of what is happening in Europe, but is not dealt with directly in the play. A strikingly harsh figure, she has developed an extreme stoicism in response to suffering. She believes that "you don't survive in dis vorld witout being like steel." She says of her experience in America, "I buried a husband and two children und I didn't cry." Nor had she cried in Germany, where "dey beat us vit sticks . . . ven ve ver children." She has been a victim, but she is also identified as a villain, and one emotionally linked with the war in Germany at the time of the play. In her home, Jay and Arty become Jakob and Artur, and they must engage in a struggle that life in America during the war might otherwise have spared them. Arty says to Jay at one point, provoking the discomfiting blend of delight and shock that are characteristic of the play, "What if one night we cut off Grandma's braids and sold it to the army for barbed wire?" The conflation here of the Jewish grandmother and the Nazi perpetrators is very telling.

⟨. . .⟩ In his 1991 review of the play, William Henry III says, "In many plays, hardened grandmothers conceal a cuddly core. Inside this woman is an iceberg, distant and adrift." The characterization of Grandma, whom Mimi Kramer singled out in her *New Yorker* review as inauthentic, and who does bear a disproportionate burden of negative qualities, is crucial to moving this theatre piece toward its dark theme, albeit slantwise.

—Bette Mandl, "Beyond Laughter and Forgetting: Echoes of the Holocaust in *Lost in Yonkers,*" *Neil Simon: A Casebook,* ed. Gary Konas (New York: Garland Publishing, Inc., 1997): pp. 70–73.

# Works by
# Neil Simon

*Phil Silvers Show* (television). 1948.

*Tallulah Bankhead Show* (television). 1951.

*Sketches.* 1952.

*Sketches,* with Danny Simon, in *New Faces of 1956.* 1956.

*Your Show of Shows* (television). 1956.

*Sid Caesar Show* (television). 1956–57.

*Jackie Gleason Show* (television). 1958–59.

*Jerry Lewis Show* (television). 1958–59.

*Red Buttons Show* (television). 1958–59.

*Sergeant Bilko* (television). 1958–59.

*Adventures of Marco Polo: A Musical Fantasy.* 1959.

*Heidi.* 1959.

*Garry Moore Show* (television). 1959–60.

*Come Blow Your Horn.* 1960.

*Little Me* (adaptation of the novel by Patrick Dennis). 1962.

*Barefoot in the Park.* 1963.

*The Odd Couple.* 1965.

*Sweet Charity* (Based on the screenplay
  *Nights of Cabria* by Federico Fellini). 1966.

*After the Fox* (screenplay). 1966.

*The Star-Spangled Girl.* 1966.

*Barefoot in the Park* (screenplay). 1967.

*The Odd Couple* (screenplay). 1968.

*Plaza Suite.* 1968.

*Promises, Promises* (Based on the screenplay
  *The Apartment* by Billy Wilder). 1968.

*Last of the Red Hot Lovers.* 1969.

*The Gingerbread Lady.* 1970.

*The Out-of-Towners* (screenplay). 1970.

*Plaza Suite* (screenplay). 1971.

*The Prisoner of Second Avenue.* 1971.

*The Comedy of Neil Simon.* 1972.

*The Heartbreak Kid* (screenplay). 1972.

*The Last of the Red Hot Lovers* (screenplay). 1972.

*The Sunshine Boys.* 1972.

*The Trouble with People* (television). 1972.

*The Good Doctor* (adaptation of stories by Chekhov). 1973.

*God's Favorite.* 1974.

*Happy Endings* (television). 1975.

*The Prisoner of Second Avenue* (screenplay). 1975.

*The Sunshine Boys* (screenplay). 1975.

*California Suite.* 1976.

*Murder By Death* (screenplay). 1976.

*The Goodbye Girl* (screenplay). 1977.

*Chapter Two.* 1977.

*California Suite* (screenplay). 1978.

*The Cheap Detective* (screenplay). 1978.

*They're Playing Our Song.* 1978.

*Chapter Two* (screenplay). 1979.

*Collected Plays 2.* 1979.

*I Ought to Be in Pictures.* 1980.

*Seems Like Old Times* (screenplay). 1980.

*Fools.* 1981.

*Brighton Beach Memoirs.* 1982.

*I Ought to Be in Pictures* (screenplay). 1982.

*Only When I Laugh* (screenplay). 1982.

*Actors and Actresses.* 1983.

*Max Dugan Returns* (screenplay). 1983.

*Biloxi Blues.* 1984.

*The Lonely Guy* (screenplay with Ed Weinberger and Stan Daniels). 1984.

*The Slugger's Wife* (screenplay). 1985.

*Broadway Bound.* 1986.

*Brighton Beach Memoirs* (screenplay). 1987.

*Biloxi Blues* (screenplay). 1988.

*Rumors.* 1988.

*Jake's Women.* 1990.

*Lost in Yonkers.* 1991.

*The Marrying Man* (screenplay). 1991.

*Broadway Bound* (television). 1992.

*Collected Plays 3.* 1992.

*Laughter on the 23rd Floor.* 1993.

*London Suite: A Comedy.* 1993.

*Lost in Yonkers* (screenplay). 1993.

*Jake's Women* (screenplay). 1996.

*Neil Simon Monologues.* 1996.

*Rewrites: A Memoir.* 1996.

*Proposals.* 1997.

*Collected Plays 4.* 1998.

*The Dinner Party.* 2000.

# Works about
# Neil Simon

Barnes, Clive. "Lost in Yonkers, Happily Ever After." *New York Post* (22 February 1991). In *New York Theatre Critics Reviews* (1991): 377–378.

———. "Theater: 'Plaza Suite,' Neil Simon's Laugh Machine." *The New York Times* (15 February 1968). In *New York Theatre Critics Reviews* (1968): 348.

Barthel, Joan. "Life for Simon—Not That Simple." *The New York Times* (25 February 1968): 2:9.

Bigsby, C. W. E. *Modern American Drama, 1945–1990.* Cambridge and New York: Cambridge University Press, 1992.

Cooke, Richard P. "Simon and Nichols Again." *The Wall Street Journal* (16 February 1968). In *New York Theatre Critics Reviews* (1968): 349.

Corry, John. "Why Broadway's Fastest Writer Cannot Slow Down." *The New York Times* (5 April 1981): 2:1.

Friedman, Samuel G., and Michaela Williams. "A Conversation Between Neil Simon and David Rabe: The Craft of the Playwright." *The New York Times Magazine* (26 May 1985): 37–38, 52, 56, 57, 60, 61, 62.

Geitner, Sheila Ennis. "Neil Simon." *Dictionary of Literary Biography,* Vol. 7: *Twentieth-Century American Dramatists.* Ed. John MacNicholas. Detroit: Gale Research Company, 1981. 252–262.

Goldman, William. *The Season: A Candid Look at Broadway.* New York: Harcourt, Brace & World, Inc., 1969.

Gottfried, Martin. "Plaza Suite." *Women's Wear Daily* (15 February 1968). In *New York Theatre Critics Reviews* (1968): 349.

———. "The Sunshine Boys." *Women's Wear Daily* (22 December 1972). In *New York Theatre Critics Reviews* (1972): 135.

Grayson, Richard. "The Fruit Brigade: Neil Simon's Gay Characters." *Neil Simon: A Casebook.* Ed. Gary Konas. New York: Garland Publishing, Inc., 1997. 137–147.

Hirschhorn, Clive. "Make 'em Laugh." *Plays and Players* 24 (September 1977): 12–15.

Johnson, Robert K. *Neil Simon.* Boston: Twayne Publishers, 1983.

Kerr, Walter. "Simon's Funny—Don't Laugh." *The New York Times* (15 February 1968). In *New York Theatre Critics Reviews* (1968): 347.

———. "What Simon Says." *The New York Times Magazine* (22 March 1970): 6, 12, 14, 16.

Kissel, Howard. "'Lost' Finds Simon in Top Form." *Daily News* (22 February 1991). In *New York Theatre Critics Reviews* (1991): 378–9.

Kroll, Jack. "Going Bonkers in Yonkers." *Newsweek* (4 March 1991). In *New York Theatre Critics Reviews* (1991): 381.

Loney, Glenn. "Simon, (Marvin) Neil." *Contemporary Dramatists,* sixth edition. Ed. Thomas Riggs. Detroit: St. James Press, 1999. 642–646.

Mandl, Bette. "Beyond Laughter and Forgetting: Echoes of the Holocaust in *Lost in Yonkers." Neil Simon: A Casebook.* Ed. Gary Konas. New York: Garland Publishing, Inc., 1997. 69–77.

McClain, John. "A Socko Comedy Success." *New York Journal American* (11 March 1965). In *New York Theatre Critics Reviews* (1965): 364.

McGovern, Edythe M. *Neil Simon: A Critical Study.* New York: Frederick Ungar Publishing Co., 1979. Updated from her previous work, *Not-So-Simple Neil Simon* (Van Nuys, CA: Perivale, 1978).

Meryman, Richard. "When the Funniest Writer in America Tried to Be Serious." *Life* (7 May 1971): 60B–60D, 64, 66–69, 71, 73, 75, 77, 79–80, 83.

Nadel, Norman. "Carney, Matthau Hilarious in *Odd Couple." The New York World-Telegram* (11 March 1965). In *New York Theatre Critics Reviews* (1965): 362.

Rich, Frank. "Simon on Love Denied." *The New York Times* (22 February 1991). In *New York Theatre Critics Reviews* (1991): 376.

Schiff, Ellen. "Funny, He *Does* Look Jewish." *Neil Simon: A Casebook.* Ed. Gary Konas. New York: Garland Publishing, Inc., 1997. 47–57.

Taubman, Howard. "Theater: Neil Simon's 'Odd Couple.'" *The New York Times* (11 March 1965). In *New York Theatre Critics Reviews* (1965): 363.

Walden, Daniel. "Neil Simon's Jewish-Style Comedies." From *Hester Street to Hollywood: The Jewish-American Stage and Screen.* Ed. Sarah Blacher Cohen. Bloomington: University of Indiana Press, 1983. 152–166.

Wilde, Larry. *How the Great Comedy Writers Create Laughter.* Chicago: Nelson-Hall, 1976.

Wilson, Edwin. "Another Winner for Neil Simon." *The Wall Street Journal* (22 December 1972). In *New York Theatre Critics Reviews* (1972): 136.

Woolf, Michael. "Neil Simon." *American Drama.* Ed. Clive Bloom. London: Macmillan, 1995. 117–130.

Zimmerman, Paul D. "Neil Simon: Up From Success." *Newsweek* (2 February 1970): 52–56.

# Index of
# Themes and Ideas

Gwendolyn Pigeon in, 16–17, 22, 23, 25; plot summary of, 14–18; pursuit of harmony in, 25–27; Roy in, 14, 19, 24; Speed in, 14, 15, 16, 19, 24; *The Sunshine Boys* compared to, 59–60; Felix Unger in, 14, 15–18, 19, 21–22, 23, 26, 27–28, 35; Vinnie in, 14, 15, 19–20, 24; wide appeal of, 16, 24–25

*ODD COUPLE, THE* (screenplay), 12

*PHIL SILVERS SHOW, THE* (television), 11

*PLAZA SUITE*, 29–47; characters in, 33–34; character verisimilitude in, 45–47; critical reception of, 12, 35–43; critical views on, 35–47, 61; Borden Eisler in, 32, 34, 43; Mr. Eisler in, 31, 32; Mimsey Hubley in, 31, 32, 34, 46; Norman Hubley in, 31–32, 34, 36, 43, 46–47; Roy Hubley in, 31, 32, 34, 36, 40, 43, 46–47; Jesse Kiplinger in, 31, 33, 36, 40, 46, 47, 61; as machine for laughing, 35–37; marriage as theme in, 39, 42; Jean McCormack in, 30, 33, 39, 42, 46; Karen Nash in, 29, 30, 33, 37, 39, 40, 42, 44, 46–47; Sam Nash in, 29–39, 33, 37, 39, 40, 42, 44, 45, 46–47, 61; plot summary of, 29–32; seriousness in comedy of, 37–38, 46, 47; sunny writing in, 43–45; Muriel Tate in, 31, 33–34, 36, 40, 42, 47; "Visitors from Forest Hills" in, 29, 31–32, 34, 35–36, 40, 42–43, 46; "Visitors from Hollywood" in, 29, 31, 33–34, 35, 36, 40, 42, 46; "Visitors from Mamaroneck" in, 29–30, 33, 35, 37, 39–40, 42, 44–45, 46; wisecrack humor in, 39–41

*PRISONER OF SECOND AVENUE, THE*, 54

*PROMISES, PROMISES*, 12

*SID CAESAR SHOW* (television), 11

SIMON, NEIL: biography of, 11–13; plays of as "period pieces," 9–10; and Yiddish theater, 9, 10

*STAR-SPANGLED GIRL, THE*, 12

*SUNSHINE BOYS, THE*, 48–62; characters in, 51; Willie Clark in, 9, 48–50, 51, 52–53, 54–55, 56, 57, 58, 61, 62; critical reception of, 48, 52–55; critical views on, 9, 10, 52–62; doctor routine in, 49–50, 53, 55, 57–58; Eddie in, 51; foibles of old age as theme in, 50, 56, 58; Jewish names in, 61–62; Al Lewis in, 9, 48, 49–50, 51, 52, 54, 55, 56, 57, 58, 61; nurse in, 50, 58; *The Odd Couple* compared to, 59–60; opposing character types in, 49, 50, 53, 55, 56, 58, 59–60; pathos in, 53, 54–56, 58; as "period piece," 9, 10; plot summary of, 48–50; Mr. Schaefer in, 51; Ben Silverman in, 48–49, 50, 51, 52, 53, 56, 58, 62; vaudeville in, 48–50, 52–53, 54, 56, 57–58, 59–60, 61–62; and Yiddish theater, 57–58, 60–62